07-CEG 60S

D0122707

THE
HIGHLY SELECTIVE
DICTIONARY
FOR THE
EXTRAORDINARILY
LITERATE

By Eugene Ehrlich:

THE HIGHLY SELECTIVE THESAURUS
FOR THE EXTRAORDINARILY LITERATE

AMO, AMAS, AMAT AND MORE

THE INTERNATIONAL THESAURUS OF QUOTATIONS
(WITH MARSHALL DEBRUHL)

THE HARPER DICTIONARY OF FOREIGN TERMS, 3RD EDITION

VENI, VIDI, VICI

MENE, MENE, TEKEL
(WITH DAVID H. SCOTT)

THE NBC HANDBOOK OF PRONUNCIATION
(WITH RAYMOND HAND, JR.)

SUPERWORDPOWER

FUNK & WAGNALLS STANDARD DICTIONARY, 2ND EDITION

OXFORD AMERICAN DICTIONARY

The

HIGHLY SELECTIVE
DICTIONARY
FOR THE
EXTRAORDINARILY
LITERATE

Introduction by
Richard Lederer

EUGENE EHRLICH

 **HarperResource**
An Imprint of HarperCollins *Publishers*

HarperCollins books may be purchased for educational, business, or sales promotional use. For information, please write to: Special Markets Department, HarperCollins Publishers, Inc., 10 East 53rd Street, New York, New York 10022.

FIRST EDITION

Library of Congress Cataloging-in-Publication Data
Ehrlich, Eugene H.
     The highly selective dictionary for the extraordinarily literate /
Eugene Ehrlich
        p. cm
     ISBN 0-06-270190-8
     1. English language—Errors of usage—Dictionaries. 2. English
language—Synonyms and antonyms.   I. Title
PE1460.E196   1997
423'.1—dc21   97-1112

02 03 04 05 ❖/RRD 20 19 18 17 16

To Norma

CONTENTS

ACKNOWLEDGMENT

Rob Amell, of HarperCollins, by his never-failing courtesy, encouragement, and cooperation, helped the editor of this dictionary accomplish his work and earned his gratitude.

PREFACE

The Highly Selective Dictionary can be thought of as an antidote to the ongoing, poisonous effects wrought by the forces of linguistic darkness—aided by permissive lexicographers who blithely acquiesce to the depredations of unrestrained language butchers.

When these permissive lexicographers perceive that journalists and other voracious consumers of Canadian wood pulp are using an existing English word in a new sense, bingo! A new definition is added to an existing dictionary entry. And—you can count on it—the addition is noticed by the lexicographic competition and is copied widely.

With what result? The functionally illiterate take this new sense as acceptable, giving them license to say, "Well, it's in the dictionary, so it's OK to use."

By contrast, *The Highly Selective Dictionary* is prescriptive, suggesting that its principal task is to define words carefully and conservatively, paying special attention to what the entry words usually mean and counseling readers not to fall for new meanings of entry words that have resulted from blunders by writers and the cooperation of permissive lexicographers.

This is not to say that new words cannot be used in writing and speaking. In fact, the English language has grown healthily over the years and is still growing at an ever-increasing rate. This is one of the reasons why English will continue to be the language of the entire world.

The Highly Selective Dictionary supplies spellings, pronunciations, and definitions for interesting words that make life rewarding for readers, writers, and public speakers. It enables users to learn the correct meanings of words they may not already know. It wastes no space on useless entries, offers a single pronunciation for most entries, and bites the bullet in pointing out confusions in the use of words.

A word must be said about the great amount of time lexicographers spend on defining common words—words whose meanings are widely known—time that could better be spent on selecting and defining entry words that readers genuinely need. While definitions supplied for common words are often admirably and ingeniously constructed, the products of this enormous effort are hundreds, if not thousands, of useless entries that do nothing for most dictionary users.

A single example of a useless entry will make clear my impatience with lexicographers. Consider the noun *door*—and who does not know what a door is? Here are the first two definitions of *door* in the great *Webster's New International Dictionary* of 1934:

1. The movable frame or barrier of boards, or other material, usually turning on hinges or pivots or sliding, by which an entranceway into a house or apartment is closed and opened; also, a similar part of a piece of furniture, as in a cabinet or bookcase.
2. An opening in the wall of a house or of an apartment, by which to go in and out; an entranceway; a doorway.

Who does not admire the scholarship and thoroughness of the lexicographer who produced these definitions? And who does not admire the latest generation of lexicographers who go on producing such definitions to this day? But who can fail to wonder why so much effort should be expended to produce them?

Finally, who are the children, women, and men who do not know what a door is and would consult a dictionary to find out?

And would the definitions given above do them any good?

The Highly Selective Dictionary for the Extraordinarily Literate, by choosing to forgo such useless entries, facilitates the reader's search for useful entries. Gone is the clutter of never-consulted entries defining words everybody knows well. Consider, for example, the paper and ink and the countless hours of word processor time and human effort devoted to defining *a, an, and, daughter, exit, promise, sky, son, sun, trouble, unfit,* and *zoo*.

Most dictionaries produced by permissive lexicographers also are willing to countenance poor pronunciations that arise from mistakes made by ill-educated radio hosts, so-called television anchorpersons, and public figures—all of them unequipped to read aloud correctly.

One example will suffice to illustrate this problem. Consider the word *nuclear*, which is not included as an entry word in the present book because it is commonly understood. We have all heard it mistakenly pronounced as NOO-kyə-lər instead of correctly as NOO-klee-ər or NYOO-klee-ər. Yet, following the principle of permissiveness, leading dictionaries sanction the mispronunciation, thereby giving solace to the bumblers—among them every member of our "nucyular navy" and most members of the U.S. Congress—who never fail to mispronounce *nuclear*.

We may have snickered when Dwight D. Eisenhower regularly mispronounced this word, and marveled at Jimmy Carter's struggles to pronounce the word correctly. Though most speakers do not aspire to high office, they can learn to speak better than most politicians.

Unfortunately, many people regard their favorite dictionary as a linguistic bible, to be accepted unquestioningly and used—along with the *Guinness Book of World Records*—in settling barroom bets. With this awesome responsibility implicitly bestowed on lexicographers, dictionaries will in time take more courageous stands on what they will sanction and what they will not.

And they may begin to overcome those who combine daily to beat our language down to a state of complete mush. Until they do, we will continue to lose good word after good word to the forces of darkness, ultimately bowing to the dictum of Lewis Carroll's Humpty Dumpty: "When *I* use a word, it means just what I choose it to mean—neither more nor less."

Eugene Ehrlich

PRONUNCIATION NOTES

The pronunciation of American English words follows few hard-and-fast rules and varies from region to region. In pronouncing the entry words of this highly selective dictionary, the editor has considered all the pronunciations given in standard sources and then tried to select the most common pronunciations. Notwithstanding, some of the pronunciations supplied indulge the editor's own preferences.

Each pronunciation is shown in parentheses just after the entry word, and the pronunciation is followed by the part of speech of the entry word. In almost all cases, only one pronunciation is given, although one of the entry words, **joust**, is given three pronunciations. When two pronunciations are considered to be equally desirable, they are connected by *or*.

For the convenience of the reader, pronunciations of the entry words employ a respelling scheme that is readily interpretable rather than the International Phonetic Alphabet, which many people find difficult to interpret.

Fully stressed syllables are shown in capital letters. Syllables that receive secondary stress are shown in small capital letters. Unstressed syllables are shown in lower case letters, as are pronunciations of words of one syllable. Three examples will suffice:

hangnail (HANG-NAYL) *noun*
infer (in-FUR) *verb*
stick (stik) *noun*

One exception to respelling is the use of the schwa (ə), which is defined as an indistinct vowel sound, as in the second syllable of **single** (SING-gəl) or in the last two syllables of **incredible** (in-KRED-ə-bəl).

Another exception to respelling is the use of ī, ī, and Ī to indicate a long vowel sound, as in **my** (mī), **finite** (FĪ-nīt), and **diagnostic** (DĪ-əg-NOS-tik).

A few additional examples will suffice to show the ease with which the supplied pronunciations can be interpreted:

abstemious (ab-STEE-mee-əs) *adjective*
accede (ak-SEED) *verb*
adduce (ə-DOOS) *verb*
adscititious (AD-si-TISH-əs) *adjective*

Two other representations of sounds depart from straightforward respelling.

As will be seen in the chart supplied below, *n* indicates an n that is only partially pronounced, as in many words of French origin.

Again, *th* is used to make the initial sound of the word "this," which is given as *th*is, and to pronounce "rather," which is given as RA*TH*-ər. In pronouncing "thin" and "both," the sound of th is not italicized.

PRONUNCIATION KEY

a *as in* **a**ct, h**a**t, c**a**rry
ah *as in* b**a**lm, c**a**lm, f**a**ther
ahr *as in* f**a**r, j**a**r, d**a**rling
air *as in* f**air**y, sc**are**, decl**are**
aw *as in* **au**dit, w**a**lk, g**aw**k, s**aw**
ay *as in* **a**ge, b**ay**, h**ei**nous
b *as in* **b**ake, **b**a**bb**le, **boob**
ch *as in* **ch**oose, **ch**ur**ch**, prea**ch**
d *as in* **d**are, fu**dd**le**d**, mu**d**

e *as in* empty, led, berry
ee *as in* ease, either, meat, see
eer *as in* ear, eerie, pier, sneer
f *as in* fin, daffy, belief
g *as in* gust, bargain, hog
h *as in* hairy, hot, huddle
hw *as in* where, whet, anywhere
i *as in* in, hit, women, twist
ī *as in* bite, light, pie, spy
ī *as in* colonize, synchronize
Ī *as in* mighty, lightning, surprise
j *as in* gin, just, judge, garbage
k *as in* kerchief, spoken, rack
l *as in* lag, ladle, sell
m *as in* many, common, madam
n *as in* note, knee, manner, napkin
n *as in* dénouement, frisson, soupçon
ng *as in* hunger, swinging, bring
o *as in* opportune, hot, crop
oh *as in* oppose, most, toast, sew
oo *as in* oodles, pool, ruler
oor *as in* poor, tour, sure
or *as in* aural, border, mortal
ow *as in* owl, oust, house, allow
oy *as in* oil, join, boy
p *as in* print, paper, sleep
r *as in* rash, tarry, poor
s *as in* cent, scent, lessen
sh *as in* sugar, shush, cash
t *as in* talk, utter, heat
th *as in* think, wrath, loath
th as in then, bother, loathe

u *as in* ugly, mutter, come
ur *as in* urge, her, fir, saboteur
uu *as in* brook, full, woman
v *as in* very, every, brave
w *as in* well, awash, allow
y *as in* yet, abeyance, useful
z *as in* zap, gazebo, tease
zh *as in* pleasure, vision, persiflage

Note: Headwords that are considered still to be foreign terms are given in italics.

INTRODUCTION

During the early years of space exploration, NASA scientist Wernher von Braun gave many speeches on the wonders and promises of rocketry and spaceflight. After one of his luncheon talks, von Braun found himself clinking cocktail glasses with an adoring woman from the audience.

"Dr. von Braun," the woman gushed, "I just loved your speech, and I found it of absolutely infinitesimal value!"

"Well then," von Braun gulped, "I guess I'll have to publish the text posthumously."

"Oh yes!" the woman came right back. "And the sooner the better!"

Now there was someone who needed to gain greater control over her word choices. But, given the power that words confer on our lives, don't we all wish to acquire a richer vocabulary? Justice Oliver Wendell Holmes once declared, "Language is the skin of living thought." Just as your skin encloses your body, so does your vocabulary bound your mental life.

It's a matter of simple mathematics: The more words you know, the more choices you can make; the more choices you can make, the more accurate, vivid, and varied your speaking and writing will be. "All words," observed Henry Ward Beecher, "are pegs to hang ideas on." Other things being equal, the larger your stock of word pegs, the closer you will come to finding the exact word that fits precisely the thought you want to express in speech or writing.

Ever since Adam assigned names to all the animals, we human beings have managed to come up with labels for almost everything on this planet—and beyond. The more of these names you acquire (and all of the italicized words that follow repose in this book), the more concise will be your expression. Why should you wheeze through a dozen words—"the act of throwing a thing or person out of a window"—when you can capture the act in a single noun: *defenestration?* Why scrawl out "a place real or imaginary where living conditions are considered to be as bad as possible," when you can capture the concept with eight little letters: *dystopia?* Wouldn't it be convenient if our language possessed a *discrete* and *discreet* word to denote the excessive development of fat on the buttocks? It does: *steatopygia.* Doesn't your heart leap up when it beholds the *effulgent* word *lambent,* at your service to describe the soft radiance of light or flame playing on a surface?

English is the most cheerfully democratic and hospitable language in the history of humankind. English has acquired the most abundant of all word stocks—616,500 entries officially enshrined in the Oxford English Dictionary, our fattest unabridged lexicon. That's an extraordinary number, considering that German owns about 185,000, so our English language boasts almost four times the number of words as the second-place language. Then come Russian at 130,000 and French at 100,000.

While there are more English words, Horatio, than are dreamt of in your philosophy, relatively few are in actual circulation. The average English speaker possesses a vocabulary of 10,000 to 20,000 words but actively uses only a small fraction, the others being recognition or recall vocabulary. A literate adult may recognize 60,000 or more words, the most learned among us 100,000. Just as we human beings use only one-tenth of our brain power, the most articulate verbivore interacts with only one-sixth of our English word hoard and actually employs only one-sixth of that.

Sadly then, many of us miss out on the sheer euphony and sesquipedalian playfulness of thousands of English words. Simply read aloud and listen to the tintinnabulation of the more ear-rinsing entries you are about to encounter: *absquatulate, anthrophagous, bumptious, concatenation, crapulous, dipsomaniac, eleemosynary, gallimaufry, glossolalia, ineluctable, legerdemain, lubricious, nugatory, peccadillo, persiflage, pinguid, plangent, pusillanimous, redolent, soporific, ululate.*

One of the happiest features of possessing a capacious vocabulary is the opportunity to insult your enemies with impunity. While the madding crowd gets mad with exhausted epithets such as "You rotten pig" and "You dirty bum," you can *acerbate, deprecate, derogate,* and *excoriate* your *nemesis* with a battalion of laser-precise *pejoratives.* You can brand him or her a *grandiloquent popinjay, venal pettifogger, nefarious miscreant, flagitious recidivist, sententious blatherskite, mawkish ditherer, arrant peculator, irascible misanthrope, hubristic narcissist, feckless sycophant, vituperative virago, vapid yahoo, eructative panjandrum, saturnine misanthrope, antediluvian troglodyte, maudlin poetaster, splenetic termagant, pernicious quidnunc, rancorous anchorite, perfidious mountebank,* or *irascible curmudgeon.*

When you were a child learning to speak, you seized each new word as if it were a shiny toy. This is how you learned your language, and this is how you can expand your vocabulary. As you keep company and build friendships with the words in *The Highly Selective Dictionary,* start using them in conversation. Encourage your children to be *beneficent* and *empathic* in their relationships. Explain to Tabby that she shouldn't be so *obdurate* about trying the latest feline cuisine. Remind yourself what an *exemplary nonpareil, indefatigable autodidact,* and *benignant thaumaturge* you are for expanding your word hoard so *perspicaciously.* Make vocabulary growth a lifelong pursuit. In the process, you will expand your thoughts and your feelings, your speaking, your reading, and your writing—everything that makes up you.

RICHARD LEDERER,
author of *Fractured English*

THE
HIGHLY SELECTIVE
DICTIONARY
FOR THE
EXTRAORDINARILY
LITERATE

A

abecedarian (AY-bee-see-DAIR-ee-ən) *noun*

1. a beginner in any field of learning.
2. a person who is learning the letters of the alphabet.

abjure (ab-JUUR) *verb*

1. repudiate, profess to abandon.
2. renounce under oath or with great solemnity.

> Some speakers and writers confuse the verbs **abjure** and **adjure**. While such confusion can readily be seen to stem from the close similarity of the spellings of the two words, it may also be related to the fact that both words are relatively uncommon. Notwithstanding, careful writers and speakers use the words correctly: **abjure** means *repudiate, renounce*, and **adjure** means *request earnestly* and *charge or command under oath or threat of penalty*. Two examples of their proper use may help: (1) "My attorney advised me to **abjure** any further action that could be construed as harassment of my ex-wife." (2) "The judge testily **adjured** the witness to speak before the jury only in response to questions put to her by the attorneys." Clear enough?

> Related words: **abjuration** (AB-jə-RAY-shən) and **abjurer** (ab-JUUR-ər) *both nouns*, **abjuratory** (ab-JUUR-ə-TOR-ee) *adjective*.

abnegate (AB-ni-gayt) *verb*

renounce, relinquish, surrender, or deny oneself (a convenience, a right, etc.).

> Related words: **abnegation** (AB-ni-GAY-shən) and **self-abnegation**, meaning self-denial, *both nouns*.

abominate (ə-BOM-ə-NAYT) *verb*
    1. abhor; regard with loathing.
    2. dislike strongly.

      Related words: **abomination** (ə-BOM-i-NAY-shən) *noun*, **abominable** (ə-BOM-ə-nə-bəl) *adjective*, **abominably** *adverb*.

abortive (ə-BOR-tiv) *adjective*
    unsuccessful, fruitless.

      Related words: **abortively** *adverb*, **abortiveness** *noun*.

absquatulate (ab-SKWOCH-ə-layt) *verb*
    1. flee; make off.
    2. abscond.

      Related words: **absquatulater** (ab-SKWOCH-ə-LAY-tər) and **absquatulation** (ab-SKWOCH-ə-LAY-shən) *nouns*.

abstemious (ab-STEE-mee-əs) *adjective*
    moderate, sparing, not self-indulgent in food and drink.

      Related words: **abstemiously** *adverb*, **abstemiousness** *noun*.

accede (ak-SEED) *verb*
    1. agree, give assent, conform.
    2. enter upon an office.

      Related words: **accedence** and **acceder** *both nouns*.

accouter (ə-KOO-tər) *verb*
    attire, equip, outfit; generally seen as **accoutered**, its past participle.

      Related word: **accouterment** (ə-KOO-tər-mənt) *noun*.

accumbent (ə-KUM-bənt) *adjective*
    reclining, recumbent.

      Related word: **accumbency** *noun*.

acerbity (ə-SUR-bi-tee) *noun*
    sharpness of speech or manner.

      Related words: **acerb** (ə-SURB) and **acerbic** *both adjectives*, **acerbate** (AS-ər-BAYT) *verb*.

Achates (ə-KAY-teez) *noun*
    a faithful companion, bosom friend; in the *Aeneid*, Achates was the faithful companion of Aeneas.

Acheron (AK-ə-ron) *noun*

the river in Hades over which Charon (KAIR-ən) ferried the souls of the dead, thus hell — called the infernal regions — itself.

adduce (ə-DOOS) *verb*

allege or cite as evidence or proof in argument.

Related words: **adduceable** and **adducible** *adjectives*, **adducer** *noun*.

adjure (ə-JUUR) *verb*

See **abjure**.

Adonis (ə-DON-is) *noun*

1. a handsome young man.
2. in classical mythology, a beautiful youth beloved by Aphrodite and killed by a boar while hunting.

adoptive (ə-DOP-tiv) *adjective*

acquired or related through adoption.

Some speakers and writers use **adopted** as a synonym for **adoptive**, thus producing incongruous phrases such as "My adopted parents," implying that *I adopted my parents*. It is preferable to use the phrase "My adoptive parents," which makes it clear that *my natural parents had given me up for adoption*.

Related word: **adoptively** *adverb*.

adscititious (AD-si-TISH-əs) *adjective*

1. supplemental, additional.
2. derived or added from an external source.

Related word: **adscititiously** *adverb*.

adumbrate (a-DUM-brayt) *verb*

1. foreshadow, prefigure.
2. overshadow.
3. shade, obscure.

Related words: **adumbrative** (a-DUM-brə-tiv) *adjective*, **adumbratively** *adverb*.

adverse (ad-VURS *or* AD-vurs) *adjective*

1. antagonistic in effect or purpose; hostile.
2. opposite, opposing, unfavorable.

Many speakers and writers confuse the adjectives **adverse** and **averse**. **Averse** means *feeling disinclined or opposed*, as in "I soon found she was **averse** to my every suggestion, and I knew I would soon be looking for a new job." Thus, resolve to be **averse** to the mistake of shielding young children from every **adverse** experience they may possibly encounter.

Related words: **adversely** (ad-VURS-lee) *adverb*, **adversity** (ad-VUR-si-tee) and **adverseness** (ad-VURS-nis) *both nouns.*

advert (ad-VURT) *verb*
1. refer to in speech or writing.
2. comment.

aegis (EE-jis) *noun*
sponsorship or protection.

affect (AF-ekt) *noun*
in psychiatry, an observed or expressed emotional response.

This noun, which has made its way into the general vocabulary of many educated people, is included here for two reasons. By far the more important reason is that the noun **affect**, when seen in print, may confuse some readers, who are familiar primarily with the verb **affect**, which is pronounced ə-FEKT and has such meanings as *produce an effect in, impress the mind, touch or move,* and *pretend or assume artificially.* In addition, the verbs **affect** and **effect**—the latter word is primarily used as a noun— are often confused by careless speakers and writers. If you doubt that any published writers fall victim to this confusion, consider that many current books, as well as a great number of today's newspapers, go to press with little, if any, editing. So you must take special care to use **affect** and **effect** correctly in your writing.

affinity (ə-FIN-i-tee) *noun, plural* **affinities**
1. a resemblance, connection, inherent agreement.
2. a natural or instinctive mutual attraction.

afflatus (ə-FLAY-təs) *noun*
1. inspiration.
2. divine impulse.

agape (AH-gah-pay) *noun, plural* **agapae** or **agapai** both pronounced AH-gah-pī
brotherly, unselfish love (contrasted with erotic love).

agent provocateur (AY-jənt prə-VOK-ə-TUR), *plural* **agents provocateurs** (AY-jənts prə-VOK-ə-TUR)

an agent hired to detect suspected persons by inciting them to commit self-incriminating acts.

aggravate (AG-rə-VAYT) *verb*

increase the gravity of (an offense, illness, problem, and the like); worsen.

Many speakers and writers use **aggravate** to mean *annoy* or *irritate*, as in "The child's incessant questioning aggravated his grandmother" and in "Don't aggravate me." They also use **aggravation** to mean *annoyance*, as in "I've had all the aggravation I can take." So prevalent have these two meanings become that most dictionaries now show them as acceptable, but usually mark these usages as colloquial. The signal for good writers is clear: If you wish to speak and write well, stay away from **aggravate** meaning *irritate* and **aggravation** meaning *annoyance*. Reserve **aggravate** for *worsen*, **aggravation** for *worsening*.

Related words: **aggravative** (AG-rə-VAY-tiv) *adjective*, **aggravator** *noun*.

agrestic (ə-GRES-tik) *adjective*

1. unpolished, awkward, uncouth.
2. rustic, rural.

aide-mémoire (AYD-mem-WAHR) *noun*, *plural* **aides-mémoire** (AYDZ-mem-WAHR)

a document, usually a memorandum, written as an aid to the memory, especially in diplomacy.

akimbo (ə-KIM-boh) *adverb*

of the arms, with hands on hips and elbows bent outward.

aleatory (AY-lee-ə-TOR-ee) *adjective*

1. depending on luck or chance.
2. especially in law, dependent on uncertain contingencies.
3. done at random, unpredictable.

Related word: **aleatoric** (AY-lee-ə-TOR-ik) *adjective*.

allocution (AL-ə-KYOO-shən) *noun*

a formal address, especially one that is hortatory in nature.

allude (ə-LOOD) *verb*

refer indirectly, covertly, or casually (to something assumed to be known).

So many speakers and writers use **allude** when they should use **refer**, which means *direct attention to by naming*, that **allude** is on the list of endangered words. For anyone who wishes to use the language carefully, **allude** for **refer** is a no-no. Example: "She **alluded** to her husband's obesity by loudly asking all the physicians at dinner whether they thought overeating was really bad for one's health." "'If you intend to **refer** to your husband's proclivities,' replied the host, 'I think you ought to pay for a consultation.'" Why abandon a word that has a useful, distinctive meaning? (See also **refer**.)

Related words: **allusion** (ə-LOO-zhən) *noun*, **allusive** (ə-LOO-siv) *adjective*, **allusively** *adverb*.

alopecia (AL-ə-PEE-shə) *noun*

baldness, whether partial or complete.

ambagious (am-BAY-jəs) *adjective*

1. circumlocutory, circuitous, roundabout.
2. tortuous.

Related words: **ambagiously** *adverb*, **ambagiousness** *noun*.

ambiguous (am-BIG-yoo-əs) *adjective*

1. open to various interpretations.
2. obscure, indistinct.

Do not confuse **ambiguous** and **ambiguity** with **ambivalent** and **ambivalence**, which see.

Related words: **ambiguously** *adverb*, **ambiguousness** and **ambiguity** (AM-bi-GYOO-i-tee) *both nouns*.

ambit (AM-bit) *noun*

1. a sphere of operation or influence.
2. precincts, bounds, scope, extent.

ambivalence (am-BIV-ə-ləns) *noun*, also given as **ambivalency**

1. uncertainty, especially when caused by inability to make up one's mind.
2. coexistence within a person of contrary tendencies or feelings.

There is a difference in the uses of **ambivalence** and **ambiguity** and the uses of their adjectival forms that is worth pointing out. **Ambivalent** is generally used to characterize the state of one's mind, while **ambiguous** is used to characterize something external to the mind. One may say, then, that people may often be **ambivalent**, but their writings should never be **ambiguous**. Again, the wording of a letter may be intentionally or unintentionally **ambiguous**, but the recipient of the letter may feel **ambivalent** toward its contents regardless of whether the letter is **ambiguous** or entirely clear, that is, **unambiguous**.

Related words: **ambivalent** *adjective*, **ambivalently** *adverb*.

amoretto (AM-ə-RET-oh) *noun, plural* **amoretti** (AM-ə-RET-ee)
a little cupid.

amphibology (AM-fə-BOL-ə-jee) and **amphiboly** (am-FIB-ə-lee) *both nouns, plurals* **amphibologies** and **amphibolies**
ambiguous speech or wording, quibble.

amphigory (AM-fi-GOR-ee) *noun, plural* **amphigories**
a nonsensical piece of verse or other writing, especially one intended as a parody.

Related word: **amphigoric** (AM-fə-GOR-ik) *adjective*.

amphora (AM-fər-ə) *noun, plural* **amphorae** (AM-fə-ree) and **amphoras**
in antiquity a two-handled Greek or Roman storage jar for oil, wine, and the like.

Related word: **amphoral** *adjective*.

anabasis (ə-NAB-ə-sis) *noun, plural* **anabases** (ə-NAB-ə-SEEZ)
a military advance, especially that of Cyrus the Younger into Asia in 401 B.C. against the forces of Artaxerxes II, as narrated by Xenophon.

anadromous (ə-NAD-rə-məs) *adjective*
of fish, migrating up rivers from the sea to spawn in fresh water.

analects (AN-əl-EKTS) and **analecta** (AN-ə-LEK-tə) *both plural nouns*
collections of literary fragments or extracts.

analogy (ə-NAL-ə-jee) *noun, plural* **analogies** (ə-NAL-ə-jeez)
a similarity between like features of two unlike things, enabling a comparison to be drawn.

Many speakers and writers, apparently perceiving **analogy** as somehow a more attractive word than **comparison**, have taken to using **analogy** as a direct synonym for **comparison**, thus thrusting **analogy** onto the precipitous path to extinction as a useful word with its own meaning. Properly, a **comparison**, not an **analogy**, is drawn between like things or persons, for example, a **comparison** of the paintings of Renoir and Degas, the baseball achievements of Roger Maris and Mickey Mantle. One may, however, draw an **analogy** between the careers of a failed artist and an unsuccessful football player, since their careers are intrinsically different.

Related words: **analogize** (ə-NAL-ə-JĪZ) *verb*; **analog** (AN-ə-LOG), **analogue**, **analogism** (ə-NAL-ə-JIZ-əm), **analogist** (ə-NAL-ə-jist), and **analogousness** (ə-NAL-ə-gəs-nis) *all nouns*; **analogous** *adjective*, **analogously** *adverb*.

Ananias (AN-ə-NĪ-əs) *noun*

1. a habitual liar.

2. in the New Testament the man who "with Sapphira his wife, sold a possession and kept back part of the price" (that is, did not give all of the proceeds to the community's common fund) and was struck dead for this act.

anaphrodisiac (an-AF-rə-DEE-zee-AK) *noun*

a drug that reduces sexual desire.

Related words: **anaphrodisia** (an-AF-rə-DEE-zhə) *noun*, **anaphrodisiac** (an-AF-rə-DEE-zee-AK) *adjective*.

anchorite (ANG-kə-RĪT) *noun*

a hermit or recluse, especially a person who has retired to a solitary place for a life of religious seclusion.

ancilla (an-SIL-ə) *noun, plural* **ancillas**

an accessory or adjunct.

ancillary (AN-sə-LER-ee) *adjective*

1. subsidiary, subordinate, subservient.

2. *(noun)* an ancilla.

3. something that serves in an ancillary capacity.

androgynous (an-DROJ-ə-nəs) *adjective*

1. hermaphroditic.

2. exhibiting both masculine and feminine characteristics.

3. neither clearly masculine nor clearly feminine.

Related word: **androgyny** (an-DROJ-ə-nee) *noun*.

anile (AN-īl) *adjective*

1. like a doddering, foolish old woman.

2. imbecilic.

Related word: **anility** (ə-NIL-i-tee) *noun*.

animadversion (AN-ə-mad-VUR-zhən) *noun*

1. the act of criticizing or censuring.

2. blame, censure, reproof.

Related words: **animdaversional** *adjective*, **animadvert** (AN-ə-mad-VURT) *verb*.

animus (AN-ə-məs) *noun*

1. strong dislike or enmity; hostility.

2. animating spirit, purpose.

3. animosity shown in action or speech.

anomalous (ə-NOM-ə-ləs) *adjective*

1. irregular.

2. abnormal.

3. not fitting into a familiar pattern of behavior; unusual.

Related word: **anomaly** (ə-NOM-ə-lee) and **anomalousness** *both nouns*.

anorexia nervosa (AN-ə-REK-see-ə nur-VOH-sə)

a symptom of emotional disturbance characterized by pathological fear of becoming fat and leading to excessive dieting.

See **bulimia**.

anserine (AN-sə-RĪN) *adjective*, also given as **anserous** (AN-sə-rəs)

1. gooselike.

2. silly, foolish; stupid.

antediluvian (AN-tee-di-LOO-vee-ən) *adjective*

old-fashioned, utterly out of date; belonging to the period before the Flood.

antepenultimate (AN-tee-pi-NUL-tə-mit) *adjective*

last but two; third from the end, especially said of a syllable.

Related word: **antepenult** (AN-tee-PEE-nult) *noun*.

anteprandial (AN-tee-PRAN-dee-əl) *adjective*, also given as **preprandial** (pree-PRAN-dee-əl)

before a meal.

anthropomorphism (AN-thrə-pə-MOR-fiz-əm) *noun*

an attribution of human form or personality to God, an animal, etc.

Related words: **anthropomorphic** *adjective*, **anthropomorphize** *verb*, **anthropomorphosis** (AN-thrə-pə-MOR-fə-sis) *noun*.

anthropophagy (AN-thrə-POF-ə-jee) *noun*

the eating of human flesh; cannibalism.

Related words: **anthropophagite** (AN-thrə-POF-ə-JĪT) *noun*; **anthropophagic** (AN-thrə-pə-FAJ-ik), **anthropophagical**, and **anthropophagous** (AN-thrə-POF-ə-gəs) *all adjectives*; **anthropophagously** *adverb*.

antipathy (an-TIP-ə-thee) *noun, plural* **antipathies**

a natural or habitual aversion.

Related words: **antipathetic** (AN-ti-pə-THET-ik) *adjective*, **antipathetically** *adverb*, **antipatheticalness** and **antipathist** (an-TIP-ə-thist) *both nouns*.

antonomasia (AN-tə-nə-MAY-zhə) *noun*

1. use of an epithet or other name in place of a proper name.
2. use of a proper name out of its original application.

Related words: **antonomastic** (AN-tə-noh-MAS-tik) and **antonomastical** *both adjectives*, **antonomastically** *adverb*.

anxious (ANGK-shəs) *adjective*

troubled, uneasy in mind; greatly worried.

Many dictionaries give **eager** as one of the meanings of **anxious**, therefore implicitly advising that the two adjectives may be used interchangeably. There is, however, good reason for keeping the two words separate, thus maintaining for **anxious** exclusive rights to *troubled, uneasy in mind* etc., while giving full privileges to **eager** in the sense of *extremely desirous*. The mingling of the two words may stem from the fact that, in sentence after sentence, a narrow difference in meaning may separate them. Think about it. Are we always sure that in a construction such as "We are anxious to see the matter settled," the state of mind of the person saying this may be construed either as *eager* or as *uneasy in mind*? Well, that depends, doesn't it? Yet, when we say we are **eager**, no reader would misconstrue the thought as expressing *anxiety*. To avoid conveying the wrong impression in your own speech and writing, therefore, choose between the two words deliberately and consistently. Remember that a home-owner who is **eager** to sell the family home may be **anxious** that potential buyers will notice the unmistakable evidence of a base-ment that floods after every heavy rain.

Related words: **anxiety** (ang-ZĪ-i-tee) and **anxiousness** *both nouns*, **anxiously** *adverb*.

apiarist (AY-pee-ə-rist) *noun*
a beekeeper.

Related words: **apiary** (AY-pee-ER-ee) *noun*, **apiarian** (AY-pee-AIR-ee-ən) *adjective*.

aplomb (ə-PLOM) *noun*
imperturbable self-possession, assurance; poise.

Apocrypha (ə-POK-rə-fə) *plural noun*
books of the Old Testament and New Testament considered not to be of inspired authorship and therefore usually omitted from Protestant editions of the Bible.

apocrypha (ə-POK-rə-fə) *plural noun*
any writings or statements of doubtful authenticity.

apocryphal (ə-POK-rə-fəl) *adjective*
1. of doubtful authenticity.
2. spurious.

Related words: **apocryphally** *adverb*, **apocryphalness** *noun*.

apodictic (AP-ə-DIK-tik) *adjective*
incontestable because clearly established or proved to be demon-strable.

Related words: **apodictical** *adjective*, **apodictically** *adverb*.

apolaustic (AP-ə-LAWS-tik) *adjective*
wholly devoted to enjoyment, seeking enjoyment.

apologia (AP-ə-LOH-jee-ə) *noun*
a written defense by a writer of his opinions or conduct.

apologue (AP-ə-LAWG) *noun*

    1. a moral fable.

    2. an allegorical story.

aposiopesis (AP-ə-SĪ-ə-PEE-sis) *noun, plural* **aposiopeses** (AP-ə-SĪ-ə-PEE-seez)

    in rhetoric, a sudden breaking off in speech, as if from inability or unwillingness to proceed.

        Related word: **aposiopetic** *adjective* (AP-ə-SĪ-ə-PET-ik).

apostasy (ə-POS-tə-see) *noun, plural* **apostasies**

    a total abandonment of one's religion, party, principles or the like.

apostate (ə-POS-tayt) *noun*

    a person who abandons his religion, party, cause or the like.

apothegm (AP-ə-THEM) *noun,* also given as **apophthegm**, pronounced identically

    a short, pithy, instructive statement.

        Related words: **apothegmatic** (AP-ə-theg-MAT-ik) and **apothegmatical** *both adjectives,* **apothegmatically** *adverb.*

apotheosis (ə-POTH-ee-OH-sis) *noun, plural* **apotheoses** (ə-POTH-ee-OH-seez)

    1. epitome, quintessence.

    2. the highest development.

    3. deification, the exaltation of a person to the rank of a god.

        Related word: **apotheosize** (ə-POTH-ee-ə-SĪZ) *verb.*

apposite (AP-ə-zit) *adjective*

    1. suitable.

    2. well expressed.

    3. pertinent.

        Related words: **appositely** *adverb,* **appositeness** *noun.*

appraise (ə-PRAYZ) *verb*

    See **apprise**.

apprise (ə-PRĪZ) *verb*

    inform, notify.

        Do not confuse **apprise** with **appraise**, which means *determine the worth of* or *put a price on* or with **appraisal**, which means *evaluation.* **Apprise** is properly used in such sentences as "Be sure to **apprise** your clients immediately when we decide to downgrade our **appraisal** of any stock."

aquiline (AK-wə-LĪN) *adjective*

    1. of or like an eagle.

    2. of a nose, curved like an eagle's beak; hooked.

    Related word: **aquilinity** (AK-wə-LIN-i-tee) *noun*.

arcane (ahr-KAYN) *adjective*

    1. mysterious, secret.

    2. obscure, esoteric.

    Related words: **arcanely** *adverb*, **arcaneness** *noun*.

archetype (AHR-ki-TĪP) *noun*

    1. a prototype.

    2. an original pattern from which copies are made.

    Related words: **archetypal** (AHR-ki-TĪ-pəl), **archetypic** (AHR-ki-TĪP-ik), **archetypical** (AHR-ki-TIP-i-kəl) *all adjectives*; **archetypally** (AHR-ki-TĪP-ə-lee) and **archetypically** (AHR-ki-TIP-ik-lee) *both adverbs*.

argot (AHR-goh) *noun*

    1. the jargon of a group or class.

    2. slang.

    Related word: **argotic** (ahr-GOT-ik) *adjective*.

Armageddon (AHR-mə-GED-ən) *noun*

    1. any great and crucial conflict.

    2. the final and completely destructive battle expected by some to be fought between nations.

    3. in the New Testament, the site of the final battle that will be fought between the forces of good and evil.

armamentarium (AHR-mə-mən-TAIR-ee-əm) *noun, plural* **armamentaria** (AHR-mə-mən-TAIR-ee-ə)

    the aggregate of equipment, techniques, and other resources available to physicians and others.

arrant (AR-ənt) *adjective*

    1. complete, unmitigated.

    2. notorious.

    Related word: **arrantly** *adverb*.

asperity (ə-SPER-i-tee) *noun, plural* **asperities**

    1. of a disposition or manner, harshness; sharpness.

    2. difficulty, hardship.

    3. unevenness or roughness of a surface.

asperse (ə-SPURS) *verb*

    attack reputation of (a person) with damaging insinuations or charges.

    Related words: **asperser** *noun,* **aspersive** *adjective,* **aspersively** *adverb.*

aspersion (ə-SPUR-zhən) *noun*

    1. derogatory or defamatory criticism.

    2. a damaging imputation.

    3. the act of defamation or slandering.

asseverate (ə-SEV-ə-RAYT) *verb*

    declare or assert earnestly or solemnly.

    Related words: **asseveration** (ə-SEV-ə-RAY-shən) *noun,* **asseverative** (ə-SEV-ə-RAY-tiv) and **asseveratory** (ə-SEV-ə-rə-TOR-ee) *both adjectives,* **asseveratively** (ə-SEV-ə-RAY-tiv-lee) *adverb.*

assiduity (AS-i-DOO-i-tee) *noun, plural* **assiduities** (AS-i-DOO-i-teez)

    1. diligence, industry.

    2. the continuing application of attention.

    Related words: **assiduous** (ə-SIJ-oo-əs) *adjective,* **assiduously** *adverb,* **assiduousness** *noun.*

assignation (AS-ig-NAY-shən) *noun*

    1. an appointment, especially a lovers' secret rendezvous.

    2. the act of assigning; an assignment.

assuage (ə-SWAYJ) *verb*

    1. make less severe.

    2. satisfy, appease.

    3. soothe, mollify.

    Related words: **assuagement** and **assuager** *both nouns.*

atavism (AT-ə-VIZ-əm) *noun*

    1. reversion to an earlier type.

    2. a reappearance of characteristics resembling those of one's grandparents or even more remote ancestors of one's parents.

Related words: **atavistic** (AT-ə-VIS-tik) *adjective*, **atavistically** *adverb*.

athanasia (ATH-ə-NAY-zhə) *noun*, also given as **athanasy** (ə-THAN-ə-see) immortality; deathlessness.

atrabilious (A-trə-BIL-yəs) *adjective*, also given as **atrabiliar** (A-trə-BIL-yər)
1. melancholy.
2. morbid.

Related word: **atrabiliousness** *noun*.

augur (AW-gər) *verb*
predict; portend.

Do not confuse **augur** with **auger**, a noun that means *a tool used in boring*. Perhaps a sentence will help you remember the difference: "The carpenter's discovery that all his **augers** had been stolen did not **augur** well for the day's work that lay before him."

auspicious (aw-SPISH-əs) *adjective*
1. propitious, favorable.
2. of good omen, promising success.

Do not confuse **auspicious** with **inauspicious**, which means *unfavorable, not of good omen*. Perhaps a sentence will help you use the two words correctly: "Morning sunshine was taken as an **auspicious** sign that the game would go well for the Yankees, but soon enough there came the **inauspicious** report that their star pitcher had a lame arm."

Related words: **auspiciously** *adverb*, **auspiciousness** *noun*.

autarchy (AW-tahr-kee) *noun*, also given as **autarky**, *plural* **autarchies** and **autarkies**
1. despotism; absolute sovereignty.
2. self-government.
3. a national policy of economic independence or self-sufficiency.

Related words: **autarchic** (aw-TAHR-kik) and **autarchical** (aw-TAHR-kə-kəl) *both adjectives*, **autarchically** *adverb*, **autarchist** (AW-tahr-kist) *noun*.

autochthon (aw-TOK-thən) *noun, plural* **autochthons** or **auto-chthones** (aw-TOK-thə-NEEZ)

> an aboriginal inhabitant of a place; an earliest known inhabitant of a place.

autochthonous (aw-TOK-thə-nəs) *adjective,* also given as **auto-chthonal** (aw-TOK-thə-nəl) and **autochthonic** (AW-tok-THON-ik)

> aboriginal, indigenous

>> Related words: **autochthonously** (aw-TOK-thə-nəs-lee) *adverb,* **autochthonism, autochthony,** and **autochthonousness** *all nouns.*

auto-da-fé (AW-toh-də-FAY) *noun, plural* **autos-da-fé** (AW-tohz-də-FAY)

> 1. the public declaration of judgment passed on persons tried in the courts of the Spanish Inquisition.
> 2. the execution by civil authorities of the sentences imposed by the courts of the Inquisition.

autodidact (AW-toh-DĪ-dakt) *noun*

> a self-taught person, especially one who has mastered a subject without benefit of formal education.

>> Related words: **autodidactic** (AW-toh-dī-DAK-tik) *adjective,* **autodidactically** (AW-toh-dī-DAK-ti-klee) *adverb.*

avarice (AV-ər-is) *noun*

> inordinate desire to acquire and hoard wealth.

>> Related words: **avaricious** (AV-ə-RISH-əs) *adjective,* **avariciously** *adverb,* **avariciousness** *noun.*

avatar (AV-ə-TAHR) *noun*

> 1. an embodiment, incarnation, or personification, as of a principle or view of life.
> 2. in Hindu mythology, the descent of a deity to earth in bodily form.

averse (ə-VURS) *adjective*

> See **adverse.**

aversion (ə-VUR-zhən) *noun*

> 1. a strong feeling of dislike or antipathy.
> 2. an object or cause of strong dislike.

3. a person strongly disliked.

Related words: **aversive** (ə-VUR-siv) *adjective*, **aversively** *adverb*, **aversiveness** *noun*.

avidity (ə-VID-i-tee) *noun*

1. eagerness, dedication, enthusiasm.
2. greediness.

Related words: **avid** (AV-id) *adjective*, **avidly** *adverb*, **avidness** *noun*.

avuncular (ə-VUNG-kyə-lər) *adjective*

of or pertaining to an uncle.

Related words: **avuncularity** (ə-VUNG-kyə-LAR-ə-tee) *noun*, **avuncularly** (ə-VUNG-kyə-lər-lee) *adverb*.

B

badinage (BAD-ə-NAHZH) *noun*
banter, humorous ridicule.

bagatelle (BAG-ə-TEL) *noun*
1. a trifle, something of little value; formerly a game resembling pinball.
2. in music, a brief, unpretentious composition, usually for piano.

bagnio (BAN-yoh) *noun, plural* **bagnios**
1. a brothel.
2. in some European countries, a bath house.

baksheesh (BAK-sheesh) *noun*
in the Near East and Middle East, a tip or gratuity; alms.

baleful (BAYL-fəl) *adjective*
1. destructive, malignant.
2. full of menacing influences.

Related words: **balefully** *adverb*, **balefulness** *noun*.

banal (bə-NAL) *adjective*
devoid of freshness, commonplace, trite.

Related words: **banality** (bə-NAL-i-tee) *noun*, **banally** (bə-NAL-ee) *adverb*.

baneful (BAYN-fəl) *adjective*
poisonous, deadly; pernicious.

Related words: **banefully** *adverb*, **banefulness** *noun*.

barbarism (BAHR-bə-RIZ-əm) *noun*

    1. a word or phrase not in accordance with normal standards; the use of such a word.

    2. an uncivilized state or condition.

    3. an instance of this.

    4. a barbarous act.

barratry (BAR-ə-tree) *noun*

    1. in law, the offense of frequently stirring up lawsuits and quarrels.

    2. in maritime law, fraud or gross criminal negligence by a captain or crew at the expense of a shipowner or of the owner of a ship's cargo.

    Related words: **barratrous** (BAR-ə-trəs) *adjective*, **barratrously** *adverb*.

basilisk (BAS-ə-lisk) *noun*

    1. in mythology, a reptile with lethal breath or look.

    2. a small tropical American lizard.

    Related words: **basiliscine** (BAS-ə-LIS-in) and **basiliscan** (BAS-ə-LIS-kən) *both adjectives*.

bastille (ba-STEEL) *noun*

    1. a fortress or prison, especially one that mistreats its convicts.

    2. a fortified tower, as of a castle.

bastinado (BAS-tə-NAH-doh) *noun*, *plural* **bastinadoes**

punishment or torture by beating on the soles of the feet.

bathos (BAY-thos) *noun*

    1. in speech or writing, a ludicrous descent from the sublime to the commonplace; an anticlimax.

    2. sentimentality, mawkishness.

    Related word: **bathetic** (bə-THET-ik) *adjective*.

bawd (bawd) *noun*

    1. a procuress.

    2. a prostitute.

beau monde (boh mawnd)

fashionable society.

behest (bi-HEST) *noun*
1. a command.
2. a strongly worded request.

belfry (BEL-free) *noun, plural* **belfries**
a bell tower, attached to a church or other structure or standing alone.

belvedere (BEL-vi-DEER) *noun*
a building designed to afford a fine view.

bemuse (bi-MYOOZ) *verb*
bewilder or befuddle (someone); stupefy.

  Related word: **bemusement** *noun*.

beneficent (bə-NEF-ə-sənt) *adjective*
1. doing good, showing kindness.
2. charitable.

  Related words: **beneficently** *adverb*, **beneficence** *noun*.

benighted (bi-NĪ-tid) *adjective*
unenlightened, ignorant.

  Related words: **benightedly** *adverb*, **benightedness** *noun*.

benignant (bi-NIG-nənt) *adjective*
1. kind, especially to subordinates or inferiors.
2. beneficial, salutary.

  Related words: **benignancy** *noun*, **benignantly** *adverb*.

besom (BEE-zəm) *noun*
a broom, especially one made of twigs or brush.

besot (bi-SOT) *verb*
1. stupefy or intoxicate, usually with drink.
2. obsess, infatuate.

bête noire (BAYT NWAHR), *plural* **bêtes noires** (BAYT NWAHRZ)
a person or thing strongly disliked or dreaded; a bane.

betide (bi-TĪD) *verb*
1. happen to (someone); befall.
2. come to pass; happen.

bhang (bang) *noun*
a narcotic and intoxicant prepared from the leaves of the Indian hemp plant.

bibelot (BIB-loh) *noun, plural* **bibelots** (BIB-lohz)
a small curio or artistic trinket.

bibulous (BIB-yə-ləs) *adjective*
addicted to *or* fond of drink.

> Related words: **bibulously** *adverb,* **bibulousness** and **bibulosity** (BIB-yə-LOS-i-tee) *both nouns.*

bifurcate (BĪ-fər-KAYT) *verb*
fork, divide into two branches.

> Related words: **bifurcate** (BĪ-fər-kit) *adjective,* **bifurcately** (BĪ-fər-KAYT-lee) *adverb,* **bifurcation** (BĪ-fər-KAY-shən) *noun.*

billingsgate (BIL-ingz-GAYT) *noun*
coarsely abusive language.

biota (bī-OH-tə) *noun*
the plant and animal life of a region.

blandish (BLAN-dish) *verb*
coax or influence by gentle flattery; cajole.

> Related words: **blandisher** and **blandishment** *both nouns,* **blandishingly** *adverb.*

blatant (BLAYT-ənt) *adjective*
1. brazenly obvious; flagrant.
2. obtrusive, tastelessly conspicuous.

> Related words: **blatantly** *adjective,* **blatancy** *noun.*

blather (BLA*TH*-ər) *noun*
foolish loquacious talk.

> Related words: **blather** *verb,* **blatherer** *noun.*

blatherskite (BLA*TH*-ər-SKĪT) *noun*
1. a person given to blathering.
2. blather; nonsense.

blench (blench) *verb*
1. draw back or flinch from; quail.
2. turn pale.

> Related words: **blencher** *noun,* **blenchingly** *adverb.*

blithe (blī*th*) *adjective*

1. merry, joyous, cheerful.
2. carefree, heedless; without thought or regard.

Related words: **blitheful** *adjective*, **blithefully** and **blithely** *both adverbs*, **blitheness** *noun*.

blithesome (BLĪ*TH*-səm) *adjective*

cheery.

Related words: **blithesomely** *adverb*, **blithesomeness** *noun*.

bloc (blok) *noun*

a group of persons, legislators, nations etc. united for a purpose.

Do not confuse **bloc** with **block**, which has many meanings, but not that of **bloc**.

bolus (BOH-ləs) *noun*, *plural* **boluses**

1. a large medicinal pill.
2. a roundish mass, especially a mass of chewed food.

boniface (BON-ə-FAYS) *noun*

an innkeeper or hotelkeeper.

bootless (BOOT-lis) *adjective*

1. unavailing, useless.
2. without result or gain.

Related words: **bootlessly** *adverb*, **bootlessness** *noun*.

boscage (BOS-kij) *noun*, also given as **boskage**

1. a mass of trees or shrubs.
2. sylvan scenery.

bosomy (BUUZ-ə-mee) *adjective*

of a woman, having a prominent bosom.

bourse (boors) *noun*

a stock exchange, especially one located in France and certain other European countries.

bowdlerize (BOHD-lə-RĪZ) *verb*

remove passages considered objectionable or vulgar from (a book etc.); expurgate.

Related words: **bowdlerism** (BOHD-lər-iz-əm), **bowdlerization** (BOHD-lər-i-ZAY-shən), and **bowdlerizer** (BOHD-lər-ĪZ-ər) *all nouns*.

brachylogy (brə-KIL-ə-jee) *noun, plural* **brachylogies**
1. conciseness or overconciseness of expression.
2. a concise or succinct expression.

braggadocio (BRAG-ə-DOH-shee-oh) *noun, plural* **braggadocios**
1. bragging, empty boasting.
2. a braggart, a boasting person.

Related word: **braggadocian** (BRAG-ə-DOH-shee-ən) *adjective*.

bravura (brə-VYUUR-ə) *noun, plural* **bravuras**
1. a brilliant performance.
2. a display of daring, especially in music.
3. a florid passage or piece requiring great skill to perform.

Related word: **bravura** *adjective*.

brigand (BRIG-ənd) *noun*
1. a member of a band of robbers living in forest or mountain regions.
2. a bandit.

Related words: **brigandage** (BRIG-ən-dij) *noun*, **brigandish** *adjective*, **brigandishly** *adverb*.

broach (brohch) *verb*
1. mention or suggest (a topic) for the first time.
2. begin drawing (beer, whiskey, etc.) as by tapping a keg or cask.

Related word: **broacher** *noun*.

bromide (BROH-mīd) *noun*
1. a platitude or trite remark.
2. a person who is unfailingly boring.

Related word: **bromidic** (broh-MID-ik) *adjective*.

brummagem (BRUM-ə-jəm) *adjective*
1. cheap and showy but inferior and worthless.
2. *(noun)* a showy but inferior thing.

brusque (brusk) *adjective*
1. blunt, offhand.
2. abrupt in manner.

Related words: **brusquely** *adverb*, **brusqueness** *noun*.

buccal (BUK-əl) *adjective*
of or pertaining to the cheek; of or in the mouth.

Related word: **buccally** *adverb*.

bucolic (byoo-KOL-ik) *adjective*, also given as **bucolical**
1. rustic, rural.
2. of or pertaining to shepherds, pastoral.

Related word: **bucolically** *adverb*.

bugaboo (BUG-ə-BOO) and **bugbear** (BUG-BAIR) *both nouns*
1. something that causes baseless fear or worry.
2. a false belief used to intimidate or dissuade.

bulimia (byoo-LIM-ee-ə) *noun*
an unnaturally persistent hunger or voracious appetite.

See **anorexia nervosa**.

Related word: **bulimic** (byoo-LIM-ik) *adjective*.

bulwark (BUUL-wərk) *noun*
1. a wall of earth or other material built for defense, rampart, fortification.
2. a protection against external danger or injury.
3. a person or principle that acts as a defense.

Related word: **bulwark** *verb*.

bumptious (BUMP-shəs) *adjective*
offensively conceited or self-assertive; pushy.

Related words: **bumptiously** *adverb*, **bumptiousness** *noun*.

burble (BUR-bəl) *verb*
1. speak at length; babble.
2. make a bubbling sound.

Related word: **burbler** *noun*.

burgeon (BUR-jən) *verb*
grow or develop rapidly; flourish.

burnish (BUR-nish) *verb*
1. polish by rubbing
2. brighten; cause to glow.

bushido (BOO-shee-DAW) *noun*

in feudal Japan, the ethical code of the samurai.

Byzantine (BIZ-ən-TEEN) *adjective*

1. complex or intricate.
2. underhanded.
3. characterized by complicated scheming and intrigue.

C

cabotage (KAB-ə-TAHZH) *noun*
1. coastal trade or navigation.
2. legal restriction of air traffic within a country's borders.

cachet (ka-SHAY) *noun, plural* **cachets** (ka-SHAYZ)
1. prestige, superior status.
2. a sign of approval, especially one given by a person who is highly regarded.
3. an official seal, as on a document.

cachexia (kə-KEK-see-ə) *noun*
general ill health causing chronic debility.

> Related word: **cachectic** (kə-KEK-tik), **cachectical**, and **cachexic** (kə-KEK-sik) *all adjectives*.

cachinnate (KAK-ə-NAYT) *verb*
laugh loudly or immoderately.

> Related words: **cachinnation** and **cachinnator** *both nouns*, **cachinnatory** (KAK-ə-nə-TOR-ee) *adjective*.

cacodemon (KAK-ə-DEE-mən) *noun*
an evil spirit or person.

> Related words: **cacodemonic** (KAK-ə-di-MON-ik) and **cacodemoniac** (KAK-ə-di-MOH-nee-AK) *both adjectives*.

cacography (kə-KOG-rə-fee) *noun*
1. bad handwriting.
2. incorrect spelling.

Related words: **cacographer** *noun*, **cacographic** (KAK-ə-GRAF-ik) and **cacographical** *both adjectives*.

cacology (kə-KOL-ə-jee) *noun*

1. bad choice of words.
2. poor pronunciation.

cairn (kairn) *noun*

a heap of stones arranged as a memorial or as a landmark.

Related words: **cairned** and **cairny** *both adjectives*.

callipygian (KAL-i-PIJ-ee-ən) *adjective*, also given as **callipygous** (KAL-i-PĪ-gəs)

having shapely buttocks.

callosity (kə-LOS-i-tee) *noun, plural* **callosities**

an abnormal hardness and thickness of the skin; a callus.

callous (KAL-əs) *adjective*

1. insensitive, unsympathetic, indifferent.
2. hardened, hard.

In rigorous adherence to the principle of descriptiveness, most conventional dictionaries have become guilty of attempted verbicide by indicating that **callus** (which see) is a noun meaning of **callous**, an adjective. In time, therefore, we can expect that most writers will be ignorant of the clear distinction between the two words that is maintained today by careful writers. Consider that until recently dictionaries identified this noun use of **callous** as a mistake in spelling, and that is how editors and writers should continue to regard it. Avoid **calluses** by learning how to type properly, not by **callous** disregard of good typing techniques.

Related words: **callously** *adverb*, **callousness** *noun*.

callus (KAL-əs) *noun, plural* **calluses**

1. a thickened part of the skin; a callosity.
2. *(verb)* form or produce a callus.

See the discussion at **callous** for guidance in differentiating the noun **callus** and the adjective **callous**.

calumniate (kə-LUM-nee-AYT) *verb*

make false and malicious statements about; slander, traduce.

Related words: **calumniation** (kə-LUM-nee-AY-shən) and **calum-niator** (kə-LUM-nee-AY-tər) *both nouns.*

calumny (KAL-əm-nee) *noun, plural* **calumnies**
1. a slander; a defamation.
2. the act of slandering.

Related words: **calumniate** (kə-LUM-nee-AYT) *verb,* **calumnia-tion** (kə-LUM-nee-AY-shən) and **calumniator** (kə-LUM-nee-AY-tər) *both nouns,* **calumnious** (kə-LUM-nee-əs) and **calumnia-tory** (kə-LUM-nee-ə-TOR-ee) *both adjectives.*

canard (kə-NAHRD) *noun*
a false report; a hoax.

cant (kant) *noun*
1. insincere use of words, especially conventional expressions of piety.
2. hypocrisy.
3. *(derogatory)* the language peculiar to a party, class, profession, or the like; jargon.
4. the private language of the underworld.

capricious (kə-PRISH-əs) *adjective*
1. subject to or indicative of whim.
2. erratic.

Related words: **capriciously** *adverb,* **caprice** (kə-PREES) and **capriciousness** *both nouns.*

captious (KAP-shəs) *adjective*
1. apt to raise objections to trivial faults or defects.
2. difficult to please.

Related words: **captiously** *adverb,* **captiousness** *noun.*

carabao (KAR-ə-BAH-oh) *noun, plural* **carabaos**
in the Philippines, the water buffalo.

The noun **carabao** is often mispronounced by people who con-fuse it with the more familiar noun **caribou**, the magnificent North American deer, which is pronounced KAR-ə-BOO.

careen (kə-REEN) *verb*
said of a vehicle in motion: lean, sway, or tip to one side.

Many speakers and writers confuse the verb **career**, meaning *proceed at full speed,* with the verb **careen**. So prevalent is this confusion that modern dictionaries commonly identify the two verbs as synonyms, thus shrinking the scope of the American language and inviting ambiguity. Fully trained editors do not encourage this confusion. Nor should you.

Related word: **careener** *verb.*

career (kə-REER) *verb*

See **careen**.

caribou (KAR-ə-BOO) *noun*

See **carabao**.

carminative (kahr-MIN-ə-tiv) *noun*
a drug curing flatulence.

Related word: **carminative** *adjective,* as in "Some **carminative** compounds may be purchased over the counter."

caseous (KAY-see-əs) *adjective*
of or like cheese.

Cassandra (kə-SAN-drə) *noun*
a person who prophesies or warns of approaching evil and is usually disregarded. In classical mythology a prophet cursed by Apollo so her prophecies, though true, were fated never to be believed.

castigate (KAS-ti-GAYT) *verb*
reprimand severely, chastise, punish.

Related words: **castigation** (KAS-ti-GAY-shən) and **castigator** (KAS-ti-GAY-tər) *both nouns,* **castigative** (KAS-ti-GAY-tiv) and **castigatory** (KAS-ti-gə-TOR-ee) *both adjectives.*

casuistry (KAZH-oo-ə-stree)
1. the application of ethical principles to cases of conscience or conduct.
2. oversubtle reasoning, quibbling, or teaching, especially in questions of morality; sophistry.

Related words: **casuist** (KAZH-oo-ist) *noun,* **casuistic** (KAZH-oo-IS-tik) and **casuistical** *both adjectives,* **casuistically** *adverb.*

catachresis (KAT-ə-KREE-sis) *noun, plural* **catachreses** (KAT-ə-KREE-seez)

incorrect use of words, as in a mistaken metaphor.

Related words: **catachrestic** (KAT-ə-KRES-tik) and **catachrestical** *both adjectives*, **catachrestically** *adverb*.

catafalque (KAT-ə-FAWK) *noun*

a raised platform on which the body of a deceased person lies or is carried in state.

catamite (KAT-ə-MĪT) *noun*

a boy or youth kept by a man for homosexual practices.

catechumen (KAT-i-KYOO-mən) *noun*

a person under instruction in the rudiments of Christianity.

Related words: **catechumenal** and **catechumenical** (KAT-i-kyoo-MEN-i-kəl) *both adjectives*, **catechumenically** *adverb*, **catechumenate** (KAT-i-KYOO-mə-NAYT) and **catechumenism** (KAT-i-KYOO-mə-niz-əm) *both nouns*.

caterwaul (KAT-ər-WAWL) *verb*

make a long wailing cry, as of a cat in rut.

Related words: **caterwaul** and **caterwauling** *both nouns*.

cavil (KAV-əl) *verb*

raise petty and irritating objections.

Related words: **cavil** and **caviler** *both nouns*, **cavilingly** *adverb*.

censer (SEN-sər) *noun*

a container in which incense is burned during a religious service.

Do not confuse **censer** with **censor**, which see.

censor (SEN-sər) *noun*

any person who exercises supervision of manners or morality.

Do not confuse **censor** with **censer**, which means *incense burner*. This confusion would appear to be merely an end product of poor spelling.

Related words: **censor** *verb*; **censorable**, **censorial** (sen-SOR-ee-əl), and **censorian** (sen-SOR-ee-ən) *all adjectives*.

cerumen (si-ROO-mən) *noun*

earwax.

Related word: **ceruminous** *adjective*.

chafe (chayf) *verb*

1. make sore by rubbing.
2. irritate or annoy.
3. become annoyed, fret.

> Do not confuse **chafe** with **chaff**, which see.

chaff (chaf) *verb*

1. tease or mock good-naturedly.
2. banter.

> Do not confuse **chaff** with **chafe**. While one of the meanings of **chafe** is *irritate*, and most people show irritation when they are **chaffed**, there is no reason to confuse the two verbs beyond their closeness of spelling. In short, when we **chaff**, meaning *tease or mock good-naturedly*, we may also **chafe**, meaning *become annoyed*, but that's the whole story.

> Related word: **chaffingly** *adverb*.

charisma (kə-RIZ-mə) *noun, plural* **charismata** (kə-RIZ-mə-tə)

a personal quality that inspires followers with devotion and enthusiasm.

> Related words: **charismatic** (KAR-iz-MAT-ik) *adjective*, **charismatize** (kə-RIZ-mə-TĪZ) *verb*.

chary (CHAIR-ee) *adjective*

1. cautious, timid, wary.
2. ungenerous; sparing of.

> Related words: **charily** *adverb*, **chariness** *noun*.

childish (CHĪL-dish) *adjective*

1. of, like, or befitting a child.
2. puerile, weak, unsuitable for an adult.

> Do not confuse **childish** with **childlike**, which see.

> Related words: **childishly** *adverb*, **childishness** *noun*.

childlike (CHILD-LĪK) *adjective*

like or befitting a child, as in innocence, meekness, or frankness.

> Be careful to maintain the distinction between **childlike** and **childish** when applying these adjectives to adults. **Childlike** is entirely complimentary, but **childish** in the sense of *unsuitable*

for an adult is pejorative. While we may be charmed by **child-like** innocence in a woman, we surely are repelled by **childish** behavior in the same woman or in any other adult. In short, we admire **childlike** innocence and we abhor temper tantrums and other **childish** behavior in a grown man or woman.

Related word: **childlikeness** *noun*.

chrestomathy (kres-TOM-ə-thee) *noun, plural* **chrestomathies**
a collection of choice literary passages, especially to help in learning a language.

Related word: **chrestomathic** (KRES-tə-MATH-ik) *adjective*.

chthonic (THON-ik) *adjective*, also given as **chthonian** (THOH-nee-ən)
dwelling in the underworld.

cicerone (SIS-ə-ROH-nee) *noun, plural* **cicerones** (SIS-ə-ROH-neez) and **ciceroni** (SIS-ə-ROH-nee)
a guide, especially for sightseers.

cicisbeo (CHEE-chiz-BAY-oh) *noun, plural* **cicisbei** (CHEE-chiz-BAY-ee)
a male escort or lover of a married woman.

Related word: **cicisbeism** (CHEE-chiz-BAY-iz-əm) *noun*.

climactic (klī-MAK-tik) *adjective*, also given as **climactical** (klī-MAK-ti-kəl)
pertaining to a climax.

Do not confuse **climactic** with **climatic**, which see.

Related word: **climactically** *adverb*.

climatic (klī-MAT-ik) *adjective*, also given as **climatical** (klī-MAT-i-kəl) and **climatal** (KLĪ-mi-təl)
pertaining to climate.

The confusion of the words **climatic** and **climactic** is usually a problem of pronunciation rather than usage. As you probably have noticed, **climatic** is frequently used mistakenly in substandard speech when **climactic**, a less commonly used adjective, conveys the intended meaning. Rarely, however, is **climactic** used when **climatic** is intended. While in published writing the confusion of **climatic**, *pertaining to climate*, and **climactic**, *per-*

taining to a climax, is seldom seen, over time the confusion will probably begin to appear in books and newspapers and should be guarded against. What we say eventually influences what we write, as any teacher of writing knows.

Related words: **climatically** *adverb.*

coeval (koh-EE-vəl) *adjective*
1. of the same age, date, or duration; equally old.
2. coincident.

Related words: **coevality** (KOH-i-VAL-i-tee) *noun,* **coevally** (koh-EE-və-lee) *adverb.*

cognizable (KOG-nə-zə-bəl) *adjective*
1. perceptible.
2. recognizable.

Related word: **cognizably** (KOG-nə-zə-blee) *adverb.*

cognizant (KOG-nə-zənt) *adjective*
aware.

collation (kə-LAY-shən) *noun*
a light meal.

colloquium (kə-LOH-kwee-əm) *noun, plural* **colloquiums** and **colloquia** (kə-LOH-kwee-ə)
an academic seminar or conference.

colloquy (KOL-ə-kwee) *noun, plural* **colloquies**
a dialogue or conversation.

Related word: **colloquist** *noun.*

colporteur (KOL-POR-tər) *noun*
a door-to-door book peddler, especially of Bibles.

comedo (KOM-i-DOH) *noun, plural* **comedos** and **comedones** (KOM-i-DOH-neez)
a blackhead.

comestibles (kə-MES-tə-bəlz) *plural noun*
articles of food; edibles.

Related word: **comestible** *adjective.*

commensurate (kə-MEN-sər-it) *adjective*
corresponding in amount, extent, or magnitude; proportionate.

Related words: **commensurately** *adverb*, **commensurateness** and **commensuration** (kə-MEN-sə-RAY-shən) *both nouns*.

commination (KOM-ə-NAY-shən) *adjective*

a threat of vengeance, especially divine vengeance.

Related words: **comminate** (KOM-ə-NAYT) *verb*, **comminator** *noun*, **comminatory** (kə-MIN-ə-TOR-ee) and **comminative** (KOM-mi-NAY-tiv) *both adjectives*.

complement (KOM-plə-mənt) *noun*

1. something that completes or makes perfect.
2. the amount or quantity required to complete something.
3. in grammar, a word or group of words added to a verb to complete the predicate.
4. *(verb)* complete; form a complement to.

Careless writers sometimes use the noun and verb **compliment** to express the meanings of the noun and verb **complement**, giving editors one more error to correct. We welcome **compliments** and are quick to **compliment** anyone who deserves such courtesies, but **compliments** and **compliment** have nothing to do with **complements**. **Complements** may be essential, but they have nothing to do with **complimenting** or paying **compliments**. Clear enough?

Related words: **complementarity** (KOM-plə-men-TAR-i-tee) *noun*, **complementary** (KOM-plə-MEN-tə-ree) *adjective*.

compliment (KOM-plə-mənt) *noun*

1. a polite expression of praise.
2. an act implying praise.
3. *(verb)* pay a compliment to.

See **complement**.

Related words: **complimentable** (KOM-plə-MEN-tə-bəl) *adjective*, **complimenter** (KOM-pli-MENT-ər) *noun*.

comprise (kəm-PRĪZ) *verb*

1. include, comprehend, consist of.
2. constitute, compose, make up.

The first definition of **comprise** given above, *include, consist of*, is considered by skilled writers and editors to be the only acceptable one. It follows the hallowed dictum "The whole *comprises* the parts." In fact, the second definition, suggesting "The parts *comprise* the whole," is widely used and has been accepted for a long time. Nevertheless, there is a strong inclination among trained editors to make the first definition the one that a careful writer should follow, and the second definition one that a careful writer should avoid. Thus, instead of writing "Players *comprise* a small army," you ought to write "Players *constitute* a small army" or "Players *make up* a small army." Following the same practice, instead of saying "A team *comprised of* dozens of specialists," you ought to write "A team *composed of* dozens of specialists."

Related words: **comprisable** *adjective*, **comprisal** *noun*.

compulsive (kəm-PUL-siv) *adjective*
1. acting as if from compulsion.
2. irresistible.

Do not confuse **compulsive** with **compulsory**, which see.

Related words: **compulsively** *adverb*, **compulsiveness** and **compulsivity** (KOM-pul-SIV-i-tee) *both nouns*.

compulsory (kəm-PUL-sə-ree) *adjective*
1. that must be done, required by the rules etc.
2. enforced.

The adjective **compulsory** has long been understood to mean *enforced*, as in **compulsory** education. It was clearly distinct in meaning from the adjective **compulsive**, which in psychological parlance means *irresistible*. With the growing influence of popular psychology, however, **compulsive** has drifted into everyday language and become confused with **compulsory**. The distinction between the two words should be maintained. Thus, **compulsory** education is required by the laws of our country, while **compulsive** gambling stems from a compulsion, an irresistible urge, to gamble. You must continue to keep these adjectives separate in your own writing, remembering that **compulsive** behavior is not mandated by law, but results from an inner urge entirely personal in nature.

Related words: **compulsorily** (kəm-PUL-sə-ri-lee) *adverb*, **compulsoriness** *noun*.

concatenate (kon-KAT-ən-AYT) *verb*
1. link together.
2. unite in a series or chain.

Related word: **concatenated** *adjective*, **concatenation** (kon-KAT-ən-AY-shən) *noun*

concinnity (kən-SIN-i-tee) *noun, plural* **concinnities**
elegance of literary structure or style.

concupiscent (kon-KYOO-pi-sənt) *adjective*
lustful or sensual; eagerly desirous.

Related words: **concupiscence** *noun*, **concupiscently** *adverb*.

condign (kən-DĪN) *adjective*
severe and well-deserved.

Related word: **condignly** *adverb*.

confabulate (kən-FAB-yə-LAYT) *verb*
converse, chat.

Related words: **confabulation** (kən-FAB-yə-LAY-shən) and **confabulator** (kən-FAB-yə-LAY-tər) *both nouns*, **confabulatory** (kən-FAB-yə-lə-TOR-ee) *adjective*.

congelation (KON-jə-LAY-shən) *noun*
1. congealing; the state of being congealed.
2. a congealed substance; a coagulation or concretion.

congenital (kən-JEN-i-təl) *adjective*
1. of a disease or physical defect, existing at birth.
2. having by nature a specified characteristic.

See also **innate**.

Related words: **congenitally** *adverb*, **congenitalness** *noun*.

congeries (KON-jə-reez) *singular* or *plural noun*
1. a mass or heap.
2. a disorderly collection.

connote (kə-NOHT) *verb*
1. of words, imply meanings or ideas beyond the explicit meaning.
2. of facts, involve as a condition or accompaniment.

See **denote**.

Related words: **connotation** (KON-ə-TAY-shən) *noun*, **connotative** (KON-ə-TAY-tiv) and **connotive** (kə-NOH-tiv) *both adjectives*, **connotatively** and **connotively** *both adverbs*.

conspectus (kən-SPEK-təs) *noun, plural* **conspectuses**

a summary, digest, or synopsis.

constitute (KON-sti-TOOT) *verb*

See **comprise**.

contemporaneous (kən-TEM-pə-RAY-nee-əs) *adjective*

existing or occurring at the same time; contemporary.

Related words: **contemporaneity** (kən-TEM-pər-ə-NEE-i-tee) and **contemporaneousness** *both nouns*, **contemporaneously** *adverb*.

continual (kən-TIN-yoo-əl) *adjective*

1. continuing over a long time without stopping or with only short breaks; intermittent.
2. always happening.

Do not confuse **continual** with **continuous**, which see.

Related word: **continually** *adverb*.

continuous (kən-TIN-yoo-əs) *adjective*

1. uninterrupted in time or sequence; continuing without a break.
2. of things, connected; unbroken.

Valid distinctions can be drawn between **continuous** and **continual** in characterizing attitudes and actions. Consider the definitions given for **continual**: 1. *continuing over a long time without stopping or with only short breaks; intermittent.* 2. *always happening.* Thus, one might correctly say, "Jack's **continual** drinking finally had taken its toll." Jack's drinking surely has been *continuing over a long time,* and just as surely as it was *always happening,* it has been *intermittent.* No one drinks anything all the time. Now consider the first definition given for **continuous**: *uninterrupted in time; continuing without a break.* Thus, one might correctly say, "The minister's **continuous** interest in his congregants' welfare is never questioned." Surely this interest was *uninterrupted in time* and *continuing without a break.* You would do well, therefore, to make **continuous** your adjective of choice for unending attitudes or actions; **continual** your adjective of choice for attitudes or actions that are interrupted from time to time.

Related word: **continuously** *adverb*.

contumacious (KON-tuu-MAY-shəs) *adjective*

1. insubordinate.
2. disobedient, especially to an order of a court.

Related words: **contumaciously** *adverb*; **contumaciousness**, **contumacity** (KON-tuu-MAS-i-tee), and **contumacy** (KON-tuu-mə-see) *all nouns*.

contumelious (KON-tuu-MEE-lee-əs) *adjective*
insolent, reproachful.

Related words: **contumeliously** *adverb*, **contumeliousness** and **contumely** (KON-tuu-mə-lee) *both nouns*.

coquette (koh-KET) *noun*
a woman who flirts with men lightheartedly.

Related words: **coquettish** *adjective*, **coquettishly** *adverb*, **coquettishness** *noun*.

corrigendum (KOR-i-JEN-dəm) *noun, plural* **corrigenda** (KOR-i-JEN-də)
a mistake to be corrected, especially an error in a printed book.

corrigible (KOR-i-jə-bəl) *adjective*

1. of faults or weaknesses, capable of being corrected or reformed; rectifiable.
2. of persons, open to correction.

Do not confuse **corrigible** with its antonym **incorrigible**, which means *unrectifiable; not open to correction*.

Related words: **corrigibility** (KOR-i-jə-BIL-ə-tee) and **corrigibleness** (KOR-i-jə-bəl-nis) *both nouns*, **corrigibly** *adverb*.

corybantic (KOR-ə-BAN-tik) *adjective*

1. frenzied.
2. agitated.

cosset (KOS-it) *verb*

1. treat as a pet.
2. coddle, pamper.

costive (KOS-tiv) *adjective*

1. constipated.
2. slow to act.
3. uncommunicative.

Related words: **costively** *adverb*, **costiveness** *noun*.

coup de grâce (koo də GRAHS) *plural*, **coups de grâce**, same pronunciation

a death blow, especially one administered as an act of mercy to a dying person.

cozen (KUZ-ən) *verb*

cheat, defraud, trick.

Related words: **cozener** *noun*, **cozeningly** *adverb*.

crapulous (KRAP-yə-ləs) *adjective*

given to, characterized by, or suffering from gross excess in eating and drinking.

Related words: **crapulously** *adverb*, **crapulousness** and **crapulosity** (KRAP-yə-LOS-i-tee) *both nouns*.

credible (KRED-ə-bəl) *adjective*

1. of a person, believable or trustworthy.
2. of a threat or warning, convincing.

Related words: **credibility** and **credibleness** *both nouns*, **credibly** *adverb*.

creditable (KRED-i-tə-bəl) *adjective*

deserving or bringing credit, reputation, esteem, etc.

Do not confuse **creditable** with **credible**, *believable*, or **credulous**, *gullible*, both of which see.

Related words: **creditableness** and **creditability** (KRED-it-ə-BIL-i-tee) *both nouns*, **creditably** *adverb*.

credulous (KREJ-ə-ləs) *adjective*

too ready to believe things, gullible.

Do not confuse **credulous** with **credible** or **creditable**, both of which see.

Related words: **credulity** (krə-DOO-li-tee) and **credulousness** (KREJ-ə-ləs-nis) *both nouns*, **credulously** *adverb*.

crevasse (krə-VAS) *noun*

a deep open crack, especially in the ice of a glacier.

Do not confuse **crevasse** with **crevice**, which means *a narrow opening or crack*.

criterion (krī-TEER-ee-ən) *noun, plural* **criteria** (krī-TEER-ee-ə) and **criterions**

1. a standard of judgment.
2. a principle for evaluating something.

When speakers or writers use **criteria** as a singular noun, they run counter to the practices of even the most permissive of lexicographers and the practices of all editors. *The criteria was considered* . . . STOP! A mistake has already been made. How did this error become so widespread in the speech and writing of the unskilled? Possibly because Latin plurals, for example, **criteria** and **errata,** lack the final letter *s* we are accustomed to in English plurals. But there may be more to it: Too many of us eagerly seize upon unfamiliar words and phrases, which somehow are thought to invest our thoughts with the appearance of learnedness. The result too often is that in doing so we make laughable errors and we appear unlearned. Remember that **criterion** is singular, and **criteria** is plural.

Related word: **criterial** (kri-TEER-ee-əl) *adjective.*

cunctation (kungk-TAY-shən) *noun*

1. delay.
2. tardiness.

Related words: **cunctatious** (kungk-TAY-shəs) and **cunctatory** (KUNGK-tə-TOR-ee) *both nouns,* **cunctative** (KUNGK-tə-tiv) *adjective.*

cupidity (kyoo-PID-i-tee) *noun*

1. excessive desire to possess something.
2. greed; avarice.

Related word: **cupidinous** (kyoo-PID-i-nəs) *adjective.*

curmudgeon (kər-MUJ-ən) *noun*

a bad-tempered, difficult person.

Related word: **curmudgeonly** *adverb.*

cynosure (SIN-ə-SHUUR) *noun*

a center of attraction or admiration.

Related word: **cynosural** (SI-nə-SHUUR-əl) *adjective*.

D

dander (DAN-dər) *noun*

1. fighting spirit.

2. loose scales formed on the skin of certain animals and shed.

dandle (DAN-dəl) *verb*

dance (a child) in one's arms or on one's knees.

Related word: **dandler** (DAN-dlər) *noun*.

dastard (DAS-tərd) *noun*

a despicable coward.

Related words: **dastard** *adjective*, **dastardliness** *noun*, **dastardly** *adjective*.

decant (di-KANT) *verb*

pour (wine etc.) gently from one container into another without disturbing the sediment.

Related words: **decanter** and **decantation** (DEE-kan-TAY-shən) *both nouns*.

decedent (di-SEE-dənt) *noun*

a dead person.

décolletage (DAY-kol-TAHZH) *noun*, also given as **decolletage**, with the same pronunciation

a low-cut neck of a dress, exposing the neck and shoulders of the wearer.

decorum (di-KOR-əm) *noun*

correctness and dignity of behavior.

decrescent (di-KRES-ənt) *adjective*

    1. decreasing gradually.

    2. waning, as the moon.

      Related word: **decrescence** *noun*.

defalcation (DEE-fal-KAY-shən) *noun*

    misappropriation of funds; the sum misappropriated.

      Related word: **defalcate** (di-FAL-kayt) *verb*.

defenestration (dee-FEN-ə-STRAY-shən) *noun*

    the act of throwing a thing or person out of a window.

definite (DEF-ə-nit) *adjective*

    clear and unmistakable; unambiguous.

      Do not confuse **definite** with **definitive**, which see.

      Related words: **definitely** *adverb*, **definiteness** *noun*.

definitive (di-FIN-i-tiv) *adjective*

    1. of a book, report, author, etc., most authoritative.

    2. finally fixing or settling something; conclusive.

      Do not confuse **definitive** with **definite**, meaning *clear and unmistakable, unambiguous*. A **definitive** edition of a work is one that has authoritative status—it is considered the last word on a topic. The adjective **definite** cannot be used to modify "edition." A **definitive** offer is one that is in final form and must be accepted or rejected without alteration of its terms. By contrast, a **definite** offer is one that is clearly stated. The mistaken use of **definitive**, meaning *most authoritative, conclusive*, instead of **definite** when the intended meaning is *unambiguous* may reflect a mind-set that leads some speakers and writers to employ words they regard as glamorous instead of staying with more common words they fully understand. Don't fall into this trap.

      Related words: **definitively** *adverb*, **definitiveness** *noun*.

deflagrate (DEF-lə-GRAYT) *verb*

    burn, especially suddenly and violently.

      Related words: **deflagrable** (DEF-lə-grə-bəl) *adjective*, **deflagrability** (DEF-lə-grə-BIL-i-tee) and **deflagration** (DEF-lə-GRAY-shən) *both nouns*.

déjà vu (DAY-zhah VOO)
1. a mistaken feeling of having experienced something that actually is encountered for the first time.
2. something tediously familiar.

deleterious (DEL-i-TEER-ee-əs) *adjective*
harmful to the body or mind; injurious.

    Related words: **deleteriously** *adverb*, **deleteriousness** *noun*.

Delilah (di-LĪ-lə) *noun*
1. a seductive and treacherous woman; a wily temptress.
2. in the Old Testament, Samson's mistress, who betrayed him to the Philistines.

delusive (di-LOO-siv) *adjective*
deceptive, misleading, raising vain hopes.

    Related words: **delusively** *adverb*, **delusiveness** *noun*.

demoniac (di-MOH-nee-ak) *adjective*, also given as **demoniacal** (DEE-mə-NĪ-ə-kəl)
1. of or like a demon.
2. possessed, as by an evil spirit.
3. frenzied, fiercely energetic.
4. **demoniac** *(noun)* a person possessed by an evil spirit.

    Related word: **demoniacally** (DEE-mə-NĪ-ik-lee) *adverb*.

demotic (di-MOT-ik) *adjective*
1. of ordinary people.
2. popular.

demulcent (di-MUL-sənt) *noun*
a soothing medicine.

    Related word: **demulcent** *adjective*.

denote (di-NOHT) *verb*
1. be the sign or symbol or name of.
2. indicate.

    See **connote**.

    Related words: **denotative** (DEE-noh-TAY-tiv) and **denotive** (di-NOH-tiv) *both adjectives*, **denotation** (DEE-noh-TAY-shən) *noun*, meaning *the explicit meaning of a word*, as distinct from its connotation.

denouement (DAY-noo-MAHN) *noun*, also given as **dénouement**, with the same pronunciation

1. the clearing up at the end of a play or story of the complications of the plot.
2. the outcome of a tangled sequence of events.

deprecate (DEP-ri-KAYT) *verb*

1. feel and express disapproval of.
2. try to turn aside (praise or blame) politely.

Do not confuse **deprecate** with **depreciate**, which see.

Related words: **deprecatingly** *adverb*, **deprecation** (DEP-ri-KAY-shən) and **deprecator** (DEP-ri-KAY-tər) *both nouns*, **deprecative** (DEP-ri-KAY-tiv) and **deprecatory** (DEP-ri-kə-TOR-ee) *both adjectives*.

depreciate (di-PREE-shee-AYT) *verb*

1. make or become lower in value.
2. disparage, belittle.

Careful writers do not use **depreciate** in its second sense, *disparage, belittle*. The confusion of **depreciate** with **deprecate** by many speakers and writers appears to reflect their familiarity with **depreciate** and their unfamiliarity with **deprecate**, which means *express disapproval of*. The two verbs are similar in spelling and fairly close in meaning—*belittle* may appear to be but one step removed from *express disapproval of*—and the more familiar word, **depreciate**, appears to be winning out. Indeed, descriptive dictionaries now treat the two words as synonyms. Careful speakers and writers, however, use both words appropriately. Prices **depreciate**; hostile critics **deprecate**. Modest people **deprecate** praise directed at them; nothing can **depreciate** deserved praise.

Related words: **depreciation** (di-PREE-shee-AY-shən) *noun*, **depreciatory** (di-PREE-shee-ə-TOR-ee) *adjective*.

deracinate (di-RAS-ə-NAYT) *verb*

uproot; isolate (someone) from his home or environment.

Related word: **deracination** (di-RAS-ə-NAY-shən) *noun*.

derision (di-RIZH-ən) *noun*

scorn, ridicule.

Related word: **derisible** (di-RIZ-ə-bəl) *adjective*.

derisive (di-RĪ-siv) *adjective*

expressing or causing derision; scornful, mocking.

See **derisory**.

Related words: **derisiveness** *noun*, **derisively** *adverb*.

derisory (di-RĪ-sə-ree) *adjective*

worthy of ridicule; too insignificant for serious consideration.

Derisory and **derisive** are close in meaning, but careful writers use the two adjectives differently. For example, something *worthy of ridicule* may be described as **derisory**, as in "Entry-level wages in our firm are **derisory**." Again, a remark *expressing derision* may be characterized as **derisive**, as in "His **derisive** comments were intended to destroy his opponent's candidacy."

derogate (DER-ə-GAYT) *verb*

detract from; disparage, belittle.

"They were known for their inclination to destroy reputations of people they worked with, but they could truthfully say they never intended to **derogate** their immediate supervisor's authority."

Related word: **derogation** (DER-ə-GAY-shən) *noun*.

derogatory (di-ROG-ə-TOR-ee) *adjective*

disparaging; contemptuous.

Related words: **derogatorily** (di-ROG-ə-TOR-ə-lee) *adverb*, **derogatoriness** (di-ROG-ə-TOR-ee-nis) *noun*.

deserts (di-ZURTS) *plural noun*

what one deserves (whether good or bad).

Do not confuse **deserts** with **desserts**, a word whose meaning we all understand. Hint: we look forward to a choice of **desserts** at the end of a good meal, but if we overeat to the point of suffering gastric pain, we are getting our just **deserts**.

desideratum (di-SID-ə-RAH-təm) *noun, plural* **desiderata** (di-SID-ə-RAH-tə)

something that is lacking but is needed or desired.

despoil (di-SPOYL) *verb*

strip of possessions; rob, pillage, plunder (a place or person).

Related words: **despoiler** and **despoilment** *both nouns*.

desuetude (DES-wi-TOOD) *noun*
a state of disuse.

detritus (di-TRĪ-təs) *noun*
1. fragments (of gravel, silt, etc.) caused by the rubbing away of a larger mass.
2. any waste; debris.

Related word: **detrital** (di-TRĪ-təl) *adjective*.

detumescence (DEE-too-MES-əns) *noun*
reduction or subsidence from a swollen state.

Related word: **detumescent** *adjective*.

devolve (di-VOLV) *verb*
pass or be passed on to a deputy or successor.

Related word: **devolvement** *noun*.

diadem (DĪ-ə-DEM) *noun*
a crown or headband worn as a sign of sovereignty.

dialectic (DĪ-ə-LEK-tik) *noun*
the investigation of the truth of opinions in philosophy, economics, etc. by systematic reasoning and logical disputation.

Related words: **dialectic**, **dialectal**, and **dialectical** *all adjectives*, **dialectician** (DĪ-ə-lek-TISH-ən) *noun*.

Diaspora (dī-AS-pər-ə) *noun*, also given as **diaspora**, especially in sense 2 below
1. the dispersion of the Jews to countries outside of Palestine after the end of the Babylonian captivity.
2. the dispersion of any minority religious or ethnic group among people of a prevailing religion or ethnicity.

dichotomy (dī-KOT-ə-mee) *noun, plural* **dichotomies**
division into two parts or kinds.

Related words: **dichotomic** (DĪ-kə-TOM-ik) and **dichotomous** (dī-KOT-ə-məs) *both adjectives*, **dichotomically** (DĪ-kə-TOM-i-klee) *adverb*, **dichotomize** (dī-KOT-ə-MĪZ) *verb*.

dictum (DIK-təm) *noun, plural* **dicta** (DIK-tə) or **dictums**
1. a formal expression of opinion, especially a judicial assertion.
2. a maxim, a saying.

diffident (DIF-i-dənt) *adjective*
lacking self-confidence; hesitating to put oneself or one's ideas forward.

Related words: **diffidence** *noun*, **diffidently** *adverb*.

dilatory (DIL-ə-TOR-ee) *adjective*
slow in doing something; not prompt; tending to procrastinate.

Related words: **dilatorily** *adverb*, **dilatoriness** *noun*.

dipsomania (DIP-sə-MAY-nee-ə) *noun*
an uncontrollable craving for alcoholic drink.

Related words: **dipsomaniac** (DIP-sə-MAY-nee-AK) *noun*, **dipso-maniacal** (DIP-sə-mə-NĪ-ə-kəl) *adjective*.

disaffected (DIS-ə-FEK-tid) *adjective*
discontented and disloyal, as toward authority.

Related words: **disaffectedly** *adverb*, **disaffectedness** *noun*.

disaffection (DIS-ə-FEK-shən) *noun*
estrangement; disloyalty; political discontent.

discomfit (dis-KUM-fit) *verb*
1. disconcert; confuse and deject.
2. thwart, foil; frustrate the plans of.

Do not confuse **discomfit** with **discomfort**, which see.

Related word: **discomfiter** *noun*.

discomfiture (dis-KUM-fi-chər) *noun*
embarrassment, confusion; frustration.

discomfort (dis-KUM-fərt) *noun*
1. uneasiness, hardship, or mild pain.
2. *(verb)* make uncomfortable or uneasy.

Do not confuse the verb **discomfort** with the verb **discomfit**. Many of today's speakers and writers are not aware at all of the word **discomfit**, and when they occasionally meet the word in a book think it is a misprint. The most assiduous of such readers may turn to a dictionary for help, but the next time they meet the word they must go back to the dictionary. Rest assured that **discomfit**, meaning *disconcert*, is still in use and serves a good purpose, as does **discomfort**, a word that gives readers and writers no trouble.

Related words: **discomfortable** *adjective*, **discomfortingly** *adverb*.

disconsolate (dis-KON-sə-lit) *adjective*

1. disappointed; unhappy at the loss of something.
2. hopelessly unhappy; gloomy; inconsolable.

Related words: **disconsolately** *adverb*, **disconsolation** (dis-KON-sə-LAY-shən) and **disconsolateness** *both nouns*.

discreet (di-SKREET) *adjective*

1. showing caution and good judgment in what one does; judicious; not giving away secrets.
2. unostentatious, not showy or obtrusive.

Do not confuse **discreet** with **discrete**, which see.

Related words: **discreetly** *adverb*, **discreetness** and **discretion** (dis-KRESH-ən) both *nouns*.

discrete (di-SKREET) *adjective*

discontinuous; detached from others; individually distinct.

Seldom can the transposition of two letters in a word create as much misunderstanding as in the mistaken use of **discrete**, *individually distinct*, in place of **discreet**, *judicious, unostentatious*, when the latter word is clearly intended. This error appears to stem from the tendency of unskilled writers to want to appear learned by using relatively uncommon words in place of common words. (Or could it merely be a keyboarding error that goes undiscovered by word processing features that check one's spelling?) Whatever the reason, **discrete** in place of **discreet** is an error that can hold a writer up to ridicule as well as to misunderstanding. Take care to avoid this confusion.

Related words: **discretely** *adverb*, **discreteness** *noun*.

disingenuous (DIS-in-JEN-yoo-əs) *adjective*

insincere, not frank; hypocritically ingenuous.

Related words: **disingenuously** *adverb*, **disingenuousness** *noun*.

disinterested (dis-IN-tə-RES-tid) *adjective*

impartial; not influenced by self-interest.

The adjective **disinterested** increasingly is misconstrued as a synonym for **uninterested**. So prevalent has this misuse become that descriptive dictionaries give *uninterested* as a second meaning of **disinterested**, although some supply the label *colloquial* for this sense, implicitly suggesting that this is the way ordinary people use the word and, perhaps, that the best speakers and writers do not accept this definition. An argument is made by descriptivists that **disinterested** historically was defined as *indifferent; not interested,* and that many people still use the word in this sense. Most careful 20th-century writers, however, choose not to accept this attitude. They find satisfaction in promoting the sense of *impartial* for **disinterested**, and you should cast your lot with them and indicate by the way you frame your sentences that you mean **disinterested** to be taken in the sense of *impartial.*

Related words: **disinterestedly** *adverb,* **disinterestedness** *noun.*

disparage (di-SPAR-ij) *verb*
belittle; speak of in a slighting way.

Related words: **disparager** and **disparagement** *both nouns,* **disparaging** *adjective,* **disparagingly** *adverb.*

disparate (DIS-pər-it) *adjective*
different in kind; without relation or comparison.

Related words: **disparately** *adverb,* **disparateness** *noun.*

dispassionate (dis-PASH-ə-nit) *adjective*
calm, impartial; free from emotion.

Related words: **dispassion** and **dispassionateness** *both nouns,* **dispassionately** *adverb.*

disquisition (DIS-kwə-ZISH-ən) *noun*
a long elaborate spoken or written account of something.

Related word: **disquisitional** *adjective.*

dissemble (di-SEM-bəl) *verb*
conceal (one's true motives or feelings); pretend.

Related words: **dissembler** *noun,* **dissemblingly** *adverb.*

dissentient (di-SEN-shənt) *adjective.*
1. dissenting, especially from the views of the majority.
2. *(noun)* a person who dissents, especially from the views of the majority.

Related words: **dissentience** and **dissentiency** *both nouns,* **dissentiently** *adverb.*

dissentious (di-SEN-shəs) *adjective*
quarrelsome; contentious.

dither (DI*TH*-ər) *verb*
1. tremble or quiver.
2. hesitate indecisively.

Related words: **ditherer** *noun*, **dithery** *adjective*.

divagate (DĪ-və-GAYT) *verb*
1. stray, wander.
2. digress.

Related word: **divagation** (DĪ-və-GAY-shən) *noun*.

doctrinaire (DOK-trə-NAIR) *adjective*
1. applying theories or principles without regard for practical considerations.
2. *(noun)* a pedantic theorist.

Related word: **doctrinairism** (DOK-trə-NAIR-iz-əm) *noun*.

dolmen (DOHL-mən) *noun*
a prehistoric structure, considered to be a tomb, with a large, relatively flat stone laid atop large upright stones.

Related word: **dolmenic** (dohl-MEN-ik) *adjective*.

dottle (DOT-əl) *noun*, also given as **dottel**
the plug of unburned tobacco left in a pipe after smoking.

dour (duur) *adjective*
gloomy; stern; obstinate.

Related words: **dourly** *adverb*, **dourness** *noun*.

doyen (dwah-YAN), **doyenne** (dwah-YEN), *both nouns, plurals* **doyens** and **doyennes**
the senior member (male **doyen**, female **doyenne**) of a body of colleagues.

dross (draws) *noun*
1. impurities; rubbish.
2. scum on molten metal.

Related words: **drossy** *adjective*, **drossiness** *noun*.

dubiety (doo-BĪ-i-tee) *noun, plural* **dubieties**; also given as **dubiosity** (DOO-bee-OS-i-tee), *plural* **dubiosities**

a feeling of doubt; a doubtful matter.

Related words: **dubious** (DOO-bee-əs) *adjective*, **dubiously** *adverb*, **dubiousness** *noun*.

dudgeon (DUJ-ən) *noun*

resentment, indignation.

dutiful (DOO-tə-fəl) *adjective*

1. showing due obedience.
2. expressive of a sense of duty.

Related words: **dutifully** *adverb*, **dutifulness** *noun*.

dysphemism (DIS-fə-MIZ-əm) *noun*

an unpleasant or derogatory word or phrase substituted for a more pleasant or less offensive one; such a substitution.

See **euphemism**.

Related word: **dysphemistic** (DIS-fə-MIS-tik) *adjective*.

dysphoria (dis-FOR-ee-ə) *noun*

a state of anxiety, unease, or mental discomfort.

Related word: **dysphoric** *adjective*.

dystopia (dis-TOH-pee-ə) *noun*

a place real or imaginary where living conditions are considered to be as bad as possible.

Related words: **dystopian** *adjective*, **dystopianism** *noun*.

E

eager (EE-gər) *adjective*

See **anxious**.

ebullient (i-BUUL-yənt) *adjective*

bubbling over with excitement or high spirits; exuberant.

> Related words: **ebullience** and **ebulliency** *both nouns,* **ebulliently** *adverb.*

éclat (ay-KLAH) *noun*

brilliant success, general applause; elaborate display.

eclectic (i-KLEK-tik) *adjective*

choosing or accepting from various sources.

> Related words: **eclectically** *adverb,* **eclecticism** (i-KLEK-tə-SIZ-əm) and **eclecticist** (i-KLEK-tə-sist) *both nouns.*

ecology (i-KOL-ə-jee) *noun*

1. the scientific study of living things in relation to each other and their environment.
2. this relationship.

> Do not confuse **ecology** with **environment**, which means *surroundings, especially those affecting people's lives.* Misuse of **ecology**—a rapidly growing phenomenon—occurs in writing as well as speech, for example, in such locutions as "Pollution is contaminating our **ecology**." Substitution of **environment** makes this sentence understandable as well as correct.

> Related words: **ecologic** (EE-kə-LOJ-ik) and **ecological** *both adjectives,* **ecologically** *adverb.*

economic (EK-ə-NOM-ik) *adjective*

1. of economics.
2. pertaining to one's own finances.

Do not confuse **economic** with **economical**, which see.

economical (EK-ə-NOM-i-kəl) *adjective*

thrifty, avoiding waste.

To set aright most succinctly the frequent confusion between **economic** and **economical**, consider the following: An **economical** person is not an **economic** person. And an **economic** historian is not an **economical** historian. Thus, **economical** has nothing to with *economics*, while **economic** has everything to do with *economics*. To conclude, writers may be **economical**, *sparing*, in their use of words, and scholars usually write **economic** tomes that may well be **uneconomical**, *unsparing*, in their use of words. So use both adjectives correctly in your own speech and writing. You will make your audience and your editors happy.

Related word: **economically** *adverb*.

edacious (i-DAY-shəs)

devouring, consuming; voracious.

Related word: **edacity** (i-DAS-i-tee) *noun*.

educe (i-DOOS) *verb*

1. bring out or develop; elicit (from a person).
2. infer (from information).

Related word: **educible** *adjective*.

effect (i-FEKT) *noun* and *verb*

See **affect**.

effective (i-FEK-tiv) *adjective*

1. powerful in its effect; producing an effect.
2. making a striking impression.
3. actual, existing; real.
4. operative, in effect.

Do not confuse **effective** with **effectual**, which see.

Related words: **effectively** *adverb*, **effectiveness** and **effectivity** (i-fek-TIV-i-tee) *both nouns*.

effectual (i-FEK-choo-əl) *adjective*
answering its purpose; sufficient to produce a desired effect.

The difference between the meanings of **effective** and **effectual** is rather subtle, but careful speakers and writers perceive this difference and choose between the two adjectives carefully. The best way to illustrate the difference is to point out that a law that is **effective** — *operative, in effect* — becomes **effectual** — *answers its purpose* — only when the law is enforced.

Related words: **effectually** *adverb*, **effectualness** and **effectuality** (i-FEK-choo-AL-i-tee) *both nouns.*

effectuate (i-FEK-choo-AYT) *verb*
cause to happen; accomplish.

Related word: **effectuation** *noun.*

effete (i-FEET) *adjective*
lacking in vitality; worn out; sterile.

Related words: **effetely** *adverb*, **effeteness** *noun.*

efficacious (EF-i-KAY-shəs) *adjective*
producing the desired result; effective as a remedy or means.

Related words: **efficaciously** *adverb*, **efficaciousness** and **efficacity** (EF-i-KAS-i-tee) *noun.*

effulgent (i-FUL-jənt) *adjective*
radiant; splendid; shining forth brilliantly.

Related words: **effulgence** *noun*, **effulgently** *adverb.*

egregious (i-GREE-jəs) *adjective*
outstandingly bad; flagrant; glaring.

Related words: **egregiously** *adverb*, **egregiousness** *noun.*

eleemosynary (EL-ə-MOS-ə-NER-ee) *adjective*
charitable; supported by charity; gratuitous.

elegy (EL-i-jee) *noun, plural* **elegies**
a sorrowful or serious poem or piece of music, especially one written as a lament for a dead person.

Do not confuse **elegy** with **eulogy**, which see.

Related words: **elegiac** (EL-i-JĪ-ək) *adjective*, **elegist** (EL-i-jist) *noun*, **elegize** (EL-i-jīZ) *verb*

elenchus (i-LENG-kəs) *noun, plural* **elenchi** (i-LENG-kī)
a logical argument that refutes another argument by proving the contrary of its conclusion.

elixir (i-LIK-sər) *noun*
an aromatic remedy believed to cure all ills.

emanate (EM-ə-NAYT) *verb*
issue or originate from a source.

> Related words: **emanative** (EM-ə-nə-TIV) and **emanatory** (EM-ə-nə-TOR-ee) *both adjectives,* **emanation** (EM-ə-NAY-shən) and **emanator** (EM-ə-NAY-tər) *both nouns.*

emasculate (i-MAS-kyə-LAYT) *verb*
1. deprive of force, especially said of writing style.
2. castrate; geld.

> Related words: **emasculate** (i-MAS-kyə-lit), **emasculative** (i-MAS-kyə-LAY-tiv), and **emasculatory** (i-MAS-kyə-lə-TOR-ee) *all adjectives;* **emasculation** (i-MAS-kyə-LAY-shən) and **emasculator** (i-MAS-kyə-LAY-tər) *both nouns.*

embrocation (EM-broh-KAY-shən) *noun*
a liquid used for rubbing on the body to relieve muscular pain, etc.

> Related word: **embrocate** (EM-broh-KAYT) *verb*

emetic (ə-MET-ik) *noun*
a medicine or other agent used to induce vomiting.

> Related words: **emetic** *adjective,* **emetically** *adverb.*

éminence grise (ay-mee-nahns GREEZ)
French: in English translated as "gray eminence," a close adviser, especially one who exercises power behind the scenes.

emollient (i-MOL-yənt) *adjective*
softening or soothing the skin.

> Related words: **emollience** and **emollient** *both nouns.*

emolument (i-MOL-yə-mənt) *noun*
a fee received; a salary.

empathy (EM-pə-thee) *noun*
the ability to identify oneself mentally with a person or thing and so understand his feelings or its meaning.

Do not confuse **empathy** with the well-known word **sympathy**, with several meanings, especially *a feeling of pity or tenderness toward one suffering pain, grief, or trouble*.

Related words: **empathetic** (EM-pə-THET-ik) and **empathic** (em-PATH-ik) *both adjectives*, **empathetically** and **empathically** *both adverbs*, **empathize** (EM-pə-THĪZ) *verb*.

encomiast (en-KOH-mee-AST) *noun*

1. a person who writes or utters an **encomium,** which see.
2. a eulogist.

Related words: **encomiastic** (en-KOH-mee-AS-tik) *adjective*, **encomiastically** *adverb*.

encomium (en-KOH-mee-əm) *noun, plural* **encomiums** and **encomia** (en-KOH-mee-ə)

high praise given in speech or writing.

endemic (en-DEM-ik) *adjective*, also given as **endemical**

1. of a disease, commonly found in a particular country or district or group of people.
2. *(noun)* such a disease.

Do not confuse **endemic** with **epidemic**, which see.

Related words: **endemically** *adverb*, **endemism** (EN-də-MIZ-əm) and **endemicity** (EN-də-MIS-i-tee) *both nouns*.

energize (EN-ər-JĪZ) *verb*

See **enervate**.

enervate (EN-ər-VAYT) *verb*

cause to lose vitality.

In poor writing and speech, the verb **enervate** often appears mistakenly in place of **energize**, a well understood verb that means *invigorate* or *give energy to*. Writers and speakers may be misled perhaps by the similarity in spelling, perhaps by the dangerous impulse to choose an uncommon word wherever a common word will do. In this case, such writers substitute an antonym for the correct word, and thus end up saying exactly the opposite of what they want to say. In your own writing, stay away from unfamiliar words unless you first check them in a dictionary. Stressing elegance in word choice can lead you down the garden path.

Related words: **enervation** (EN-ər-VAY-shən) and **enervator** (EN-ər-VAY-tər) *both nouns,* **enervative** (EN-ər-VAY-tiv) *adjective.*

engender (en-JEN-dər) *verb*
give rise to; beget.

Related words: **engenderer** and **engenderment** *both nouns.*

ennui (ahn-WEE) *noun*
a feeling of mental weariness from lack of interest; boredom.

enormity (i-NOR-mi-tee) *noun, plural* **enormities**
1. great wickedness.
2. a serious crime or error.

The noun **enormity** is used frequently with the meaning of *enormous size* or *immensity.* Whatever the historical justification for this definition, the use of **enormity** in this sense starts the other meanings of this valuable word down the path to extinction. While it easy to see the confusion of **enormousness** with **enormity,** careful writers and speakers do not fall into this trap. Nor should you. Use **enormity** in discussing heinous crimes, **immensity** in discussing great size.

enormousness (i-NOR-məs-nis) *noun*
See **enormity.**

entreat (en-TREET) *verb*
request earnestly or emotionally; beseech.

Related words: **entreatingly** *adverb,* **entreatment** and **entreaty** *both nouns.*

enviable (EN-vee-ə-bəl) *adjective*
desirable enough to arouse envy.

Do not confuse **enviable** with the more common adjective **envious,** meaning *full of envy.* Thus, we write "She has an **enviable** reputation," not an **envious** reputation. Writers who mistakenly use these words interchangeably—a definite no-no—are held in low regard by editors and intelligent readers.

Related words: **enviableness** *noun,* **enviably** *adverb.*

envious (EN-vee-əs) *adjective*
See **enviable.**

environment (en-VĪ-rən-mənt) *noun*

    See **ecology**.

ephemeral (i-FEM-ər-əl) *adjective*

    lasting only a very short time; transitory.

        Related words: **ephemerally** *adverb*, **ephemerality** (i-FEM-ə-RAL-i-tee) and **ephemeralness** (i-FEM-ər-əl-nis) *both nouns.*

epicene (EP-i-SEEN) *adjective*

    1. belonging to, or sharing the characteristics of, both sexes; of no definite sex or kind.

    2. effeminate; unmasculine.

        Related word: **epicenism** (EP-i-SEEN-iz-əm) *noun.*

epicure (EP-i-KYUUR) *noun*

    See **gourmet**.

epidemic (EP-i-DEM-ik) *adjective*

    1. of a disease, spreading rapidly through a community where the disease is not always prevalent, infecting many persons at the same time.

    2. *(noun)* such a disease.

        Do not confuse **epidemic** with **endemic**. The word **epidemic** is in common use and well known, but **endemic**, as an adjective meaning *commonly found in a particular country or district or group of people*, is less frequently used and is most likely to be used correctly by knowledgable epidemiologists. Try to remember.

        Related words: **epidemically** *adverb*, **epidemicity** (EP-i-də-MIS-i-tee) *noun.*

epigone (EP-i-GOHN) *noun, plural* **epigones** and **epigoni** (e-PI-goh-nī); the singular form is also given as **epigon** (EP-i-GON), *plural* **epigons**

    an undistinguished imitator or descendant of an illustrious person or family.

        Related words: **epigonic** (EP-i-GON-ik) *adjective*, **epigonism** (i-PIG-ə-NIZ-əm) *noun.*

epiphany (i-PIF-ə-nee) *noun, plural* **epiphanies**

    1. a manifestation, as of God; usually, a manifestation of Christ as divine.

2. a sudden, intuitive insight into the essential meaning of something.

Related words: **epiphanic** (EP-ə-FAN-ik) and **epiphanous** (i-PIF-ə-nəs) *both adjectives*.

epistolary (i-PIS-tə-LER-ee) *adjective*
contained in or carried on by letters; of or pertaining to letters.

epitaph (EP-i-TAF) *noun*
See **epithet**.

epithet (EP-ə-THET) *noun*
1. a descriptive word or phrase.
2. a contemptuous word or phrase.

Do not confuse **epithet** with the well-understood **epitaph**, meaning *words inscribed on a tomb or describing a dead person*. While **epitaph** is almost never used incorrectly, **epithet** frequently appears incorrectly in student themes.

Related words: **epithetic** (EP-i-THET-ik) and **epithetical** (EP-i-THET-i-kəl) *both adjectives*.

epitome (i-PIT-ə-mee) *noun*
1. something that shows on a small scale the qualities of something larger.
2. a person who embodies a quality.

Epitome does not mean *the best*, even though many people think this is one of the word's meanings. Use the word only as defined above, for example, "She is the **epitome** of grace."

Related words: **epitomic** (EP-i-TOM-ik) and **epitomical** (EP-i-TOM-i-kəl) *both adjectives*, **epitomize** (i-PIT-ə-MĪZ) *verb*.

eponym (EP-ə-nim) *noun*
a person whose name is taken for a people, place, institution, etc.

Related words: **eponymic** (EP-ə-NIM-ik) and **eponymous** (ə-PON-ə-məs) *both adjectives*, **eponymy** (ə-PON-ə-mee) *noun*.

equable (EK-wə-bəl) *adjective*
1. uniform, unvarying.
2. even-tempered.

Do not confuse **equable** with **equitable**, which see.

Related words: **equability** (EK-wə-BIL-i-tee) and **equableness** (EK-wə-bəl-nis) *both nouns*, **equably** *adverb*.

equitable (EK-wi-tə-bəl) *adjective*

fair and just.

> Do not confuse **equitable** with **equable**, meaning *uniform, unvarying; even-tempered*. A legal claim may be **equitable**; a region's weather conditions and a person's temperament may be **equable**.

> Related words: **equitableness** *noun*, **equitably** *adverb*.

equivocal (i-KWIV-ə-kəl) *adjective*

1. able to be interpreted in two ways; ambiguous.
2. of doubtful nature or character; questionable; suspicious.

> Related words: **equivocacy** (i-KWIV-ə-kə-see), **equivocality** (i-KWIV-ə-KAL-i-tee), and **equivocalness** (i-KWIV-ə-kəl-nis) *all nouns*; **equivocally** *adverb*.

equivocate (i-KWIV-ə-KAYT) *verb*

1. use ambiguous words in order to conceal the truth.
2. tell lies.

> Related words: **equivocatingly** (i-KWIV-ə-KAYT-ing-lee) *adverb*, **equivocation** (i-KWIV-ə-KAY-shən) and **equivocator** (i-KWIV-ə-KAY-tər) *both nouns*.

equivoque (EK-wə-VOHK) *noun*, also given as **equivoke**

1. a play on words; a pun.
2. ambiguity.

eremite (ER-ə-MĪT) *noun*

a hermit or recluse, especially one who has taken religious vows.

> Related words: **eremitic** (ER-ə-MIT-ik), **eremitical** (ER-ə-MIT-i-kəl), and **eremitish** (ER-ə-MĪ-tish) *all adjectives*; **eremitism** (ER-ə-MIT-iz-əm) *noun*.

eructation (i-ruk-TAY-shən) *noun*

1. belching.
2. discharge of a volcano.

> Related words: **eruct** (i-RUKT) and **eructate** (i-RUK-tayt) *both verbs*, **eructative** (i-RUK-tə-tiv) *adjective*.

eschew (es-CHOO) *verb*
    avoid; abstain from.

>   Related words: **eschewal** and **eschewer** *both nouns*.

escritoire (ES-kri-TWAHR) *noun*
    a writing desk with drawers.

esoteric (ES-ə-TER-ik) *adjective*
    intended only for people with special knowledge or interest; not
        generally intelligible.

>   Do not confuse **esoteric** with **exoteric**, which see.

>   Related words: **esoterica** (ES-ə-TER-i-kə) *noun*, **esoterically**
    adverb.

esurient (i-SUUR-ee-ənt) *adjective*
    1. hungry.
    2. greedy.

>   Related words: **esurience** and **esuriency** *both nouns*, **esuriently**
    adverb.

ethos (EE-thos) *noun*
    the characteristic spirit and beliefs of a community, person, or liter-
        ary work.

etiology (EE-tee-OL-ə-jee), *plural* **etiologies**
    1. the study of causes, as in philosophy, physics, etc.
    2. the assignment of cause, especially in disease.

>   Related word: **etiologist** *noun*.

eulogy (YOO-lə-jee) *noun*, *plural* **eulogies**; also given as **eulogium**
(yoo-LOH-jee-əm), *plural* **eulogiums** and **eulogia** (yoo-LOH-jee-ə)
    a speech or piece of writing in praise of a person, especially a
        funeral oration; praise.

>   Do not confuse **eulogy** with **elegy**, meaning *sorrowful music or*
    poetry, especially a piece written as a lament for a dead person.
    The distinction is that a **eulogy**—not an **elegy**—is given at a
    funeral or memorial service and, particularly in modern times,
    may be cast as a message of general hope or of genial good
    humor.

>   Related words: **eulogist** *noun*, **eulogize** (YOO-lə-jīz) *verb*.

euphemism (YOO-fə-MIZ-əm) *noun*

a mild or roundabout expression substituted for one considered offensive, too harsh, or too blunt.

Do not confuse **euphemism** with **euphuism**, which see.

Related words: **euphemist** *noun*; **euphemistic** (YOO-fə-MIS-tik), **euphemistical**, and **euphemious** (yoo-FEE-mee-əs) *all adjectives*; **euphemistically** and **euphemiously** *both adverbs*.

euphuism (YOO-fyoo-IZ-əm) *noun*

1. an artificial or affected style of writing.
2. high-flown language.

Do not confuse **euphuism**, *an affected style*, with **euphemism**, *a roundabout expression*. The former is considered excessively ornate, the latter inappropriately indirect, in contrast with modern writing, which values calling a spade a spade.

Related words: **euphuist** *noun*, **euphuistic** (YOO-fyoo-IS-tik) and **euphuistical** (YOO-fyoo-IS-ti-kəl) *both adjectives*, **euphuistically** (YOO-fyoo-IS-ti-klee) *adverb*.

exacerbate (ig-ZAS-ər-BAYT) *verb*

make (pain, disease, anger, etc.) worse; aggravate.

Related words: **exacerbatingly** (ig-ZAS-ər-BAYT-eeng-lee) *adverb*, **exacerbation** (ig-ZAS-ər-BAY-shən) *noun*.

excoriate (ik-SKOR-ee-AYT) *verb*

1. denounce, reproach harshly.
2. remove part of the skin by abrasion; strip or peel off (skin).

Related word: **excoriation** (ik-SKOR-ee-AY-shən) *noun*.

exculpate (EK-skul-PAYT) *verb*

free (a person) from blame; clear of a charge of wrongdoing; exonerate.

Related words: **exculpable** (ik-SKUL-pə-bəl) and **exculpatory** (ik-SKUL-pə-TOR-ee) *both adjectives*, **exculpation** (EK-skul-PAY-shən) *noun*.

execrable (EK-si-krə-bəl) *adjective*

very bad; abhorrent, detestable, abominable.

Related words: **execrableness** *noun*, **execrably** *adverb*.

execrate (EK-si-KRAYT) *verb*
    detest greatly; denounce; utter curses upon.

        Related words: **execration** (EK-si-KRAY-shən) and **execrator** (EK-si-KRAY-tər) *both nouns*; **execrative** (EK-si-KRAY-tiv) and **execratory** (EK-si-krə-TOR-ee) *both adjectives*.

exegesis (EK-si-JEE-sis) *noun, plural* **exegeses** (EK-si-JEE-seez)
    critical exposition or interpretation of a text, especially of Scripture.

        Related words: **exegetic** (EK-si-JET-ik) and **exegetical** *both adjectives*.

exegete (EK-si-JEET) *noun*, also given as **exegetist** (EK-si-JET-ist)
    a person skilled in exegesis.

exemplar (ig-ZEM-plahr) *noun*
    1. a worthy model or pattern.
    2. a typical example.

exemplary (ig-ZEM-plə-ree) *adjective*
    1. very good, an example to others.
    2. serving as an example.

        Related words: **exemplarily** (ig-ZEM-plə-rə-lee) *adverb*, **exemplariness** and **exemplarity** (IG-zem-PLAR-i-tee) *both nouns*.

exemplify (ig-ZEM-plə-FLĪ) *verb*
    serve as an example of.

        Related words: **exemplifiable** (ig-ZEM-plə-FĪ-ə-bəl) and **exemplificative** (ig-ZEM-plə-fi-KAY-tiv) *both adjectives*, **exemplification** (ig-ZEM-plə-fi-KAY-shən) and **exemplifier** (ig-ZEM-plə-FĪ-ər) *both nouns*.

exequies (EK-si-kweez) *noun plural; singular* **exequy**
    funeral rites; obsequies.

exhaustive (ig-ZAWS-tiv) *adjective*
    trying all possibilities; thorough.

        Do not confuse **exhaustive** with **exhausted** or **exhausting**, which are used primarily to mean *fatigued* and *fatiguing* respectively. An **exhaustive** search means a *thorough search*, not a *tiring search*.

        Related words: **exhaustively** *adverb*, **exhaustiveness** *noun*.

existentialism (EG-zi-STEN-shə-LIZ-əm) *noun*

a philosophical theory emphasizing that a person is responsible for his own actions and free to choose his development and destiny.

Related words: **existential** *adjective*, **existentialist** *adjective* and *noun*, **existentially** *adverb*.

exoteric (EK-sə-TER-ik) *adjective*

1. understandable by outsiders.
2. commonplace, popular.

Do not confuse **exoteric** with **esoteric**, which means *intended only for people with special knowledge or interest*. Thus, **esoteric** is used to characterize knowledge or information that may be possessed by persons on the inside, **exoteric** to characterize knowledge or information that is widely available.

Related words: **exoterically** *adverb*, **exotericism** (EK-sə-TER-i-siz-əm) *noun*.

expatiate (ik-SPAY-shee-AYT) *verb*

speak or write about (a subject) at great length or in detail.

Related words: **expatiation** (ik-SPAY-shee-AY-shən) and **expatiator** (ik-SPAY-shee-AY-tər) *both nouns*.

expiate (EK-spee-AYT) *verb*

make amends for (wrongdoing); atone.

Related words: **expiable** (EK-spee-ə-bəl) and **expiatory** (EK-spee-ə-TOR-ee) *both adjectives*, **expiation** (EK-spee-AY-shən) and **expiator** (EK-spee-AY-tər) *both nouns*.

explicate (EK-spli-KAYT) *verb*

1. make clear.
2. explain (a literary work etc.); interpret.

Related words: **explicable** (EK-spli-kə-bəl), **explicative** (EK-spli-kə-tiv), and **explicatory** (EK-spli-kə-TOR-ee) *all adjectives*; **explication** (EK-spli-KAY-shən) and **explicator** (EK-spli-KAY-tər) *both nouns*.

expostulate (ik-SPOS-chə-LAYT) *verb*

1. make a friendly protest.
2. reason or argue with a person.

Related words: **expostulatingly** (ik-SPOS-chə-LAYT-ing-lee) *adverb*, **expostulation** (ik-SPOS-chə-LAY-shən) and **expostulator** (ik-SPOS-chə-LAY-tər) *both nouns*, **expostulatory** (ik-SPOS-chə-lə-TOR-ee) *adjective*.

expunge (ik-SPUNJ) *verb*

wipe or rub out; erase; delete.

Related word: **expunger** *noun*.

expurgate (EK-spər-GAYT) *verb*

1. purify (a book etc.) by removing objectionable matter.
2. remove (such matter).

Related works: **expurgation** (EK-spər-GAY-shən) and **expurgator** (EK-spər-GAY-tər) *both nouns*.

extenuate (ik-STEN-yoo-AYT) *verb*

make (a person's guilt or offense) seem less by providing a partial excuse.

Related words: **extenuating** and **extenuative** (ik-STEN-yoo-AY-tiv) *both adjectives*, **extenuatingly** *adverb*, **extenuator** *noun*.

extirpate (EK-stər-PAYT) *verb*

root out and destroy completely.

Related words: **extirpation** (EK-stər-PAY-shən) and **extirpator** (EK-stər-PAY-tər) *both nouns*, **extirpative** (EK-stər-PAY-tiv) *adjective*.

extrinsic (ek-STRIN-sik) *adjective*

1. originating from outside.
2. not essential or inherent; extraneous.
Related word: **extrinsically** *adverb*.

F

factious (FAK-shəs) *adjective*
1. having factions.
2. creating dissension; turbulent.

Do not confuse **factious** with **factitious**, which see.

Related words: **factiously** *adverb*, **factiousness** *noun*.

factitious (fak-TISH-əs) *adjective*
1. made for a special purpose.
2. not genuine, contrived, artificial.

Do not confuse **factitious** with its look-alike, **factious**. **Factious** has meanings related to *factions*. **Factitious** suggests *manufacture*; *contrivance* and *artificiality*.

Related words: **factitiously** *adverb*, **factitiousness** *noun*.

fainéant (FAY-nay-ahn) *noun*, also given as **faineant** (FAY-nee-ənt)
1. an idler.
2. *(adjective)* idle, indolent.

Related words: **fainéance** *noun*, also given as **faineance** (FAY-nee-əns).

fakir (fə-KEER) *noun*, also given as **fakeer**
a Muslim or Hindu religious beggar regarded as a holy man.

Do not confuse **fakir** with **faker**, *someone who tries to deceive people*.

famous (FAY-məs) *adjective*
See **notorious**.

farrago (fə-RAH-goh) *noun, plural* **farragos** or **farragoes**
a confused mixture; a medley, a hodgepodge.

> Related word: **farraginous** (fə-RAJ-ə-nəs) *adjective*.

fascicle (FAS-i-kəl) *noun*
1. one section of a book that is published in installments.
2. in botany, a small bundle or tight cluster.

> Related words: **fascicular** (fə-SIK-yə-lər) and **fasciculate** (fə-SIK-yə-lit) *both adjectives*, **fasciculation** (fə-SIK-yə-LAY-shən) *noun*.

fatidic (fay-TID-ik) *adjective*, also given as **fatidical** (fay-TID-i-kəl)
1. prophetic.
2. possessing prophetic power.

> Related word: **fatidically** *adverb*.

fatuous (FACH-oo-əs) *adjective*
1. foolish, silly; purposeless.
2. unreal.

> Related words: **fatuitous** (fə-TOO-i-təs) *adjective*; **fatuity** (fə-TOO-i-tee), **fatuitousness**, and **fatuousness** (FACH-oo-əs-nis) *all nouns*; **fatuously** (FACH-oo-əs-lee) *adverb*.

fealty (FEE-əl-tee) *noun, plural* **fealties**
loyalty; fidelity.

febrifuge (FEB-rə-FYOOJ) *noun*
a cooling drink or medicine to reduce fever.

> Related word: **febrifugal** (FEB-rə-FYOO-gəl) *adjective*.

febrile (FEB-rəl) *adjective*
feverish.

> Related word: **febrility** (fi-BRIL-i-tee) *noun*.

feckless (FEK-lis) *adjective*
feeble and incompetent; irresponsible.

> Related words: **fecklessly** *adverb*, **fecklessness** *noun*.

feculent (FEK-yə-lənt) *adjective*
full of dregs or fecal matter; turbid; foul; stinking.

> Related word: **feculence** *noun*.

fecund (FEE-kənd) *adjective*
fertile; prolific.

> Related word: **fecundity** (fi-KUN-di-tee) *noun*.

feisty (FĪ-stee) *adjective*
1. exuberant; spirited; spunky.
2. pugnacious; aggressive; ill-tempered.
3. troublesome; difficult.

> Related words: **feistily** (FĪST-i-lee) *adverb*, **feistiness** *noun*.

fell (fel) *adjective*
1. ruthless, cruel, savage.
2. destructive.

> Related word: **fellness** *noun*.

feral (FER-əl) *adjective*
1. wild, untamed.
2. in a wild state after escape from captivity.

fervid (FUR-vid) *adjective*
ardent, intense; fervent.

> Related words: **fervidity** (fur-VID-i-tee) *noun*, **fervidly** (FUR-vid-lee) *adverb*.

fetid (FET-id) *adjective*
stinking.

> Related words: **fetidly** *adverb*, **fetidness** and **fetidity** (fe-TID-i-tee) *both nouns*.

fictive (FIK-tiv) *adjective*
1. imaginary; fictitious.
2. related to the creation of fiction.

> Related word: **fictively** *adverb*.

flagitious (flə-JISH-əs) *adjective*
deeply criminal; utterly villainous.

> Related words: **flagitiously** *adverb*, **flagitiousness** *noun*.

flatulent (FLACH-ə-lənt) *adjective*
1. causing or suffering from the formation of gas in the intestinal tract.

2. pretentious; windy, puffed up.

Related words: **flatulence** and **flatulency** *both nouns*, **flatulently** *adverb*.

flaunt (flawnt) *verb*

display oneself or one's possessions ostentatiously.

Do not confuse **flaunt** with **flout**, which see.

Related words: **flaunter** *noun*, **flauntingly** *adverb*.

fledged (flejd) *adjective*

1. of young birds, with fully grown wing feathers; able to fly.
2. mature, trained, and experienced.

fleer (fleer) *verb*

laugh impudently or mockingly; jeer, deride.

Related words: **fleer** *noun*, **fleeringly** (FLEER-ing-lee) *adverb*.

flotsam (FLOT-səm) *noun*

1. debris or wreckage found floating on the water.
2. **flotsam and jetsam**, tramps, vagrants, etc.; odds and ends.

See **jetsam**.

flounder (flown-dər) *verb*

1. move clumsily and with difficulty, as in mud.
2. make mistakes or become confused when trying to do something.

Do not confuse **flounder** with **founder**, which see.

Related word: **flounderingly** *adverb*.

flout (flowt) *verb*

1. disobey openly and scornfully.
2. mock; express scorn for.

Careless writers and speakers, encouraged by the siren call of permissive dictionaries, may use **flaunt**, meaning *display ostentatiously*, when **flout**, meaning *express scorn for*, is the meaning intended. While this misuse is often seen, perhaps because the two verbs are close in pronunciation, it should be avoided. Here is a sentence that will help you remember the principal meanings of the two verbs: "People **flaunt** their ignorance when they **flout** established principles of good writing and speech."

Related words: **flouter** *noun*, **floutingly** *adverb*.

forceful (FORS-fəl) *adjective*

powerful and vigorous; effective; impressive

Do not confuse **forceful** with **forcible**, which see.

Related words: **forcefully** *adverb*, **forcefulness** *noun*.

forcible (FOR-sə-bəl) *adjective*

accomplished by force.

Some dictionaries treat **forceful** as one of the meanings of **forcible**, since people more and more use **forcible** in this sense. Notwithstanding, it is worthwhile to maintain the distinction between the two words. Careful writers and speakers use **forceful** in the sense of *powerful and vigorous*, **forcible** in the sense of *accomplished by force*. When inspired, most of us can deliver a **forceful** speech, but only a felon or an authorized person—for example, a police officer or a firefighter—can ever make a **forcible** entry.

Related words: **forcibleness** and **forcibility** (FOR-sə-BIL-ə-tee) *both nouns*, **forcibly** *adverb*.

forswear (for-SWAIR) *verb*

1. give up.
2. renounce, especially under oath.
3. **forswear oneself**, swear falsely, commit perjury.

Related word: **forswearer** *noun*.

forte (fort) *noun*

a person's strong point.

The pronunciation of **forte** as FOR-tay is frequently heard but must be considered incorrect except when **forte** is intended as a term in music, with the meaning of *loud* or *loudly*.

forthcoming (FORTH-KUM-ing) *adjective*

1. about to appear; approaching.
2. made available or produced when needed.
3. willing to give information; responsive.

Related word: **forthcomingness** *noun*.

forthwith (FORTH-WITH) *adverb*
without delay; immediately.

fortuitous (for-TOO-i-təs) *adjective*
happening by chance; accidental.

> **Fortuitous** is rapidly losing the meanings given above, with most writers and speakers preferring to use this adjective to mean *lucky*. The adjective they appear to have in mind—if indeed they think about what they are saying—is **fortunate**. So widespread is this rape of **fortuitous** that *lucky* or its equivalent is now given by many dictionaries as a second meaning of this otherwise excellent, unambiguous adjective. Careful writers and speakers resist this misguided use of **fortuitous**, but maybe they are fighting a losing battle. In your own work, fight the good fight to preserve **fortuitous** and keep editors happy.

> Related words: **fortuitously** *adverb*, **fortuitousness** and **fortuity** (for-TOO-i-tee) *both nouns*.

fortunate (FOR-chə-nit) *adjective*
See **fortuitous**.

founder (FOWN-dər) *verb*
1. of a ship, fill with water and sink.
2. fail completely.

> **Flounder**, meaning *move clumsily and with difficulty*, is sometimes confused with **founder**, meaning *fail completely* and *fill with water and sink*. Undoubtedly, the similarity in spelling of the two verbs does not make life easy for careless writers and speakers, but the distinction between **founder** and **flounder** should be retained. Remember that you and I can **flounder** helplessly until we get our bearings, and while ships, political parties, organizations, and the like can also **flounder** as they try to make their way through difficult situations, when they are going down for the count, they are **foundering**. And that's as final as things can get.

fractious (FRAK-shəs) *adjective*
irritable, peevish; unruly.

> Do not confuse **fractious** with **factious**, which has the meaning *creating tension*. The two words are so nearly identical in

spelling that this confusion is understandable. But who ever said good writing is easy? Above all, don't become **fractious** when you must deal with **factious** people.

Related words: **fractiously** *adverb*, **fractiousness** *noun*.

frangible (FRAN-jə-bəl) *adjective*
breakable, fragile.

Related words: **frangibility** (FRAN-jə-BIL-i-tee) and **frangibleness** (FRAN-jə-bəl-nis) *both nouns.*

fratricide (FRA-tri-sīD) *noun*
1. the act of killing one's brother or sister.
2. a person who commits this crime.

Related word: **fratricidal** (FRA-tri-SĪD-əl) *adjective.*

frenetic (frə-NET-ik) *adjective*
frantic; frenzied.

Related word: **frenetically** *adverb.*

friable (FRĪ-ə-bəl) *adjective*
easily crumbled, crumbly.

Related words: **friability** (FRĪ-ə-BIL-i-tee) and **friableness** (FRĪ-ə-bəl-nis) *both nouns.*

frisson (free-SAWN) *noun, plural* **frissons** (free-SAWNZ)
1. an emotional thrill.
2. a shudder of emotion.

frowzy (FROW-zee) *adjective*, also given as **frowsy** (FROW-zee)
1. ill-smelling or musty.
2. unkempt; slovenly.

Related words: **frowzily** (FROW-zi-lee) *adverb*, **frowziness** *noun.*

fugacious (fyoo-GAY-shəs) *adjective*
1. fleeting, transitory.
2. difficult to capture.

Related words: **fugaciousness** and **fugacity** (fyoo-GAS-i-tee) *both nouns*, **fugaciously** *adverb.*

fulsome (FUUL-səm) *adjective*
cloying, excessive, disgusting.

Fulsome is an example of a word with a well-defined and useful meaning that is in danger of being lost because many writers use the word loosely, and permissive lexicographers write their definitions based on how writers use words rather than how writers should use words. Thus, because many uninformed writers, who may view **fulsome** as a synonym for **full**, use **fulsome** to convey the meaning of *copious* or *abundant*, modern dictionaries often include this sense in writing their definitions. While there is controversy over this use of **fulsome**, there is little doubt today that informed writers and their editors wish to preserve the meaning of **fulsome** as *cloying, excessive,* and *disgusting*. At the same time, because of the need to avoid ambiguity in your writing, you ought to use **fulsome** only to convey the meanings given above, and make it clear you do not mean *copious* or *abundant*.

Related words: **fulsomely** *adverb*, **fulsomeness** *noun*.

G

galimatias (GAL-ə-MAY-shee-əs) *noun*
confused or unintelligible talk.

gallimaufry (GAL-ə-MAW-free) *noun, plural* **gallimaufries**
a jumble or medley; a hodgepodge.

gambit (GAM-bit) *noun*
1. an opening move in chess in which a player intentionally sacrifices a pawn or other piece in order to gain an advantage.
2. a maneuver, especially in conversation, that is intended to secure an advantage.

gastronome (GAS-trə-NOHM) *noun*
a connoisseur of good eating and drinking.

> Related words: **gastronomic** (GAS-trə-NOM-ik) and **gastronomical** *both adjectives,* **gastronomically** *adverb,* **gastronomist** (ga-STRON-ə-mist) and **gastronomy** (ga-STRON-ə-mee) *both nouns.*

gauche (gohsh) *adjective*
1. lacking in ease and grace of manner; awkward.
2. tactless.

> Related words: **gauchely** *adverb,* **gaucheness** *noun.*

gaucherie (GOH-shə-REE) *noun, plural* **gaucheries** (GOH-shə-REEZ)
1. a gauche action.
2. gauche manners.

gelid (JEL-id) *adjective*
icy, ice-cold; chilly.

Related words: **gelidity** (jə-LID-i-tee) and **gelidness** (JEL-id-nis) *both nouns*, **gelidly** (JEL-id-lee) *adverb*.

genuflect (JEN-yuu-FLEKT) *verb*

1. bend the knee and lower the body, especially in reverence.
2. show servility.

Related words: **genuflection** (JEN-yuu-FLEK-shən) and **genuflector** (JEN-yuu-FLEK-tər) *both nouns*.

gibbet (JIB-it) *noun*

a gallows; an upright post with an arm from which the bodies of executed criminals were formerly suspended.

gloaming (GLOH-ming) *noun*

the evening twilight; dusk.

glossolalia (GLAW-sə-LAY-lee-ə) *noun*

the power of speaking in unknown languages as claimed by religious groups in ecstatic worship; the gift of tongues.

Related word: **glossolalist** (glaw-SOL-ə-list) *noun*

gnosis (NOH-sis) *noun*

1. knowledge of spiritual mysteries.
2. mystical knowledge.

Related words: **gnostic** (NOS-tik) *adjective* and *noun*, **gnostical** (NOS-ti-kəl) *adjective*, **gnostically** *adverb*.

gourmand (guur-MAHND) *noun*

1. a lover of food.
2. a glutton.

Do not confuse **gourmand** with **gourmet**, which see.

Related words: **gourmandize** (GUUR-mən-DĪZ) *verb*, **gourmandise** (GUUR-mən-DEEZ) and **gourmandism** (GUUR-mən-diz-əm) *both nouns*.

gourmet (guur-MAY) *noun*

a connoisseur of good food and drink; an epicure; a gastronome.

Good writers and speakers do not use **gourmet** and **gourmand** as synonyms, even though many dictionaries bow to those who do not observe this distinction by supplying **gourmet** as one meaning of **gourmand**. It is important to be able to differentiate these two words, as even these same dictionaries implicitly do, since they stop short of supplying **gourmand** as one meaning of **gourmet**. Of course, their reason for doing so surely reflects the much less common use of **gourmand**, making it unlikely that writers will use **gourmand** mistakenly, if at all. As a careful writer, you ought to reserve **gourmand** for a person who can best be described as a *glutton*, **gourmet** for a person who can best be described as a *connoisseur of good food and drink* or *epicure*.

grabble (GRAB-əl) *verb*

1. feel or search with the hands; grope about.
2. sprawl on all fours; scramble for.

Related word: **grabbler** *noun*.

gracile (GRAS-il) *adjective*

slender, thin; gracefully slender.

Related words: **gracility** (gra-SIL-i-tee) and **gracileness** (GRAS-il-nis) *both nouns*.

grandiloquent (gran-DIL-ə-kwənt) *adjective*

1. using pompous language.
2. given to boastful talk.

Related words: **grandiloquence** *noun*, **grandiloquently** *adverb*.

gratuitous (grə-TOO-i-təs) *adjective*

1. given or done without good reason.
2. given or done without payment; free, unearned.

Related words: **gratuitously** *adverb*, **gratuitousness** *noun*.

grisette (gri-ZET) *noun*

a young French workingwoman, especially a seamstress or shop assistant.

Related word: **grisettish** *adjective*.

Grundyism (GRUN-dee-IZ-əm) *noun*

1. a narrow-minded adherence to conventionality, combining propriety and prudery in matters of personal behavior.
2. **grundyism**, an instance of such conventionalism.

Mrs. Grundy, a character created by English playwright Thomas Morton in his play *Speed the Plough* (1798), personifies the tyrannical constraints of conventional opinion in matters of propriety. Although Mrs. Grundy does not appear in the play, her presence is strongly felt when her name repeatedly comes up in the question "What will Mrs. Grundy say?" The modern counterpart of this question is our own "What will the neighbors say?"

Related words: **Grundyist** and **Grundyite** (GRUN-dee-īt) *both nouns.*

gudgeon (GUJ-ən) *noun*
1. a small freshwater fish used as bait.
2. a credulous person.
3. a dupe.

H

habitué (hə-BICH-oo-AY) *noun, plural* **habitués**
    one who visits a place regularly.

hagiography (HAG-ee-OG-rə-fee) *noun, plural* **hagiographies**
    the writing and study of the lives of saints.

        Related words: **hagiographer** (HAG-ee-OG-rə-fər) *noun,* **hagiographic** (HAG-ee-ə-GRAF-ik) and **hagiographical** *both adjectives.*

halcyon (HAL-see-ən) *adjective,* less frequently given as **halcyonian** (HAL-see-OH-nee-ən) and **halcyonic** (HAL-see-ON-ik)
    1. calm and peaceful.
    2. happy and prosperous.

harbinger (HAHR-bin-jər) *noun*
    a person, event, or thing that announces the approach of another;
      a forerunner; an omen.

harridan (HAR-i-dən) *noun*
    a bad-tempered old woman; a shrew.

haruspex (hə-RUS-peks) *noun, plural* **haruspices** (hə-RUS-pə-SEEZ)
    in ancient Rome, a priest who practiced divination, especially by
      examining the entrails of dead animals; a soothsayer.

        Related words: **haruspicy** (hə-RUS-pə-see) and **haruspication** (hə-RUS-pi-KAY-shən) *both nouns,* **haruspical** (hə-RUS-pi-kəl) *adjective.*

hauteur (hoh-TUR) *noun*
    1. haughtiness of manner.
    2. arrogance.

healthful (HELTH-fəl) *adjective*

    1. conducive to good health.

    2. beneficial; salutary.

        Do not confuse **healthful** with **healthy**, which see.

        Related words: **healthfully** *adverb*, **healthfulness** *noun*.

healthy (HEL-thee) *adjective*

    1. having or showing good health.

    2. prosperous or sound.

        In discussing climate, diet, and other factors affecting health, our best writers and speakers employ **healthful** in the sense of *conducive to good health*. In describing a person, situation, business etc. showing health, our best writers employ **healthy** in the sense of *having or showing good health* or, as appropriate, *prosperous or sound*. So widespread is the confusion of **healthy** with **healthful** that—you guessed it—permissive lexicographers sprinkle holy water on this example of poor usage by treating the two words as synonyms. There is little hope of reversing this trend, but you will do yourself no harm by continuing to maintain the separate meanings of **healthful** and **healthy**. In doing so, you will mark yourself as a careful writer by continuing to have a **healthy** respect for the English language and do yourself a lot of good by following **healthful** practices in your daily life.

        Related words: **healthily** *adverb*, **healthiness** *noun*.

hebdomedal (heb-DOM-ə-dəl) *adjective*

    weekly.

        Related word: **hebdomadally** *adverb*.

hebetude (HEB-i-TOOD) *noun*

    dullness, obtuseness; lethargy.

        Related words: **hebetate** (HEB-i-TAYT) *verb*, **hebetudinous** (HEB-i-TOO-də-nəs) *adjective*.

hector (HEK-tər) *verb*

    1. intimidate by bullying; bully.

    2. treat with insolence.

hegemony (hi-JEM-ə-nee) *noun, plural* **hegemonies**

    1. dominance of leadership, especially by one nation over another.

2. leadership, predominance.

Related words: **hegemonic** (HEJ-ə-MON-ik) and **hegemonical** *both adjectives*, **hegemonism** (hi-JEM-ə-NIZ-əm) and **hegemonist** (hi-JEM-ə-nist) *both nouns*.

hegira (hi-JĪ-rə) *noun*, also given as **hejira**, with the same pronunciation, and as **hijra** (HIJ-rə)

1. a journey undertaken to escape danger or to enjoy a more congenial place.

2. **Hijra**, the flight of Muhammad to Medina in A.D. 622.

heinous (HAY-nəs) *adjective*
very wicked, odious; outrageous; totally reprehensible.

Related words: **heinously** *adverb*, **heinousness** *noun*.

henotheism (HEN-ə-thee-IZ-əm) *noun*
the belief in one god as the deity of one's family or tribe without disbelieving in the existence of other gods.

Related words: **henotheist** (HEN-ə-THEE-ist) *noun*, **henotheistic** (HEN-ə-thee-IS-tik) *adjective*.

hermeneutics (HUR-mə-NOO-tiks) *noun*
the art or science of interpretation, especially of Scripture.

Related words: **hermeneutic** and **hermeneutical** *both adjectives*.

heteroclite (HET-ər-ə-KLĪT) *adjective*, also given as **heteroclitic** (HET-ər-ə-KLIT-ik) and **heteroclitical**

1. abnormal or irregular.

2. *(noun)* a person or thing that deviates from what is considered normal.

heterodox (HET-ər-ə-DOKS) *adjective*
not in accordance with accepted doctrines or opinions; unorthodox.

Related words: **heterodoxly** *adverb*, **heterodoxy** *noun*.

heuristic (hyuu-RIS-tik) *adjective*

1. serving to discover.

2. pertaining to a trial-and-error method of computer problem solving.

Related word: **heuristically** *adverb*.

hircine (HUR-sīn) *adjective*

    1. goatlike.

    2. lustful.

historic (hi-STOR-ik) *adjective*

    1. well-known or important in history.

    2. making history, momentous.

    Do not confuse **historic** with **historical**, which see.

historical (hi-STOR-i-kəl) *adjective*

    1. belonging to or dealing with history or past events.

    2. concerned with history.

    Despite the willingness of some lexicographers to accept **historic** as a synonym for **historical**, the two words carry separate and useful meanings worth preserving. Consider that publication of a **historical** novel—*one that deals with past events*, whether factual or not—can intrigue us or leave us flat, but it seldom can achieve celebrity worthy of a place in history. On the other hand, a **historic** event—*one that has made history*—finds a place in history regardless of whether a novel is published that is based on the event. Again, a **historical** novel can achieve widespread readership even though it may not be based on a **historic** event, indeed even if it is based on an event that is actually the product of a novelist's imagination. Thus, you are advised to use this pair of adjectives as suggested here. **Historic** events may or may not become subjects of **historical** fiction.

    Related word: **historically** *adverb*, **historicalness** *noun*.

histrionic (HIS-tree-ON-ik) *adjective*

    1. of actors or acting.

    2. dramatic or theatrical in manner.

    Related word: **histrionically** *adverb*.

histrionics (HIS-tree-ON-iks) *noun, plural* or *singular*

dramatic behavior intended to impress people.

homunculus (hə-MUNG-kyə-ləs) *noun, plural* **homunculi** (hə-MUNG-kyə-lī)

    1. a little man.

    2. a manikin, a dwarf.

Related word: **homuncular** *adjective*.

honorific (ON-ə-RIF-ik) *noun*

1. an expression implying respect.
2. a mark of esteem.

Related words: **honorific** and **honorifical** *both adjectives*, **honorifically** *adverb*.

hortative (HOR-tə-tiv) and **hortatory** (HOR-tə-TOR-ee) *both adjectives*

1. serving or tending to exhort.
2. encouraging.

Related words: **hortation** (hor-TAY-shən) *noun*, **hortatively** (HOR-tə-tiv-lee) and **hortatorily** (HOR-tə-TOR-i-lee) *both adverbs*.

hotelier (OH-tel-YAY) *noun*

a hotelkeeper.

houri (HUUR-ee) *noun, plural* **houris**

1. a beautiful and voluptuous woman.
2. a beautiful virgin provided in paradise for each faithful Muslim.

hoyden (HOYD-ən) *noun*, also given as **hoiden**

1. a boisterous, carefree girl.
2. a tomboy.

Related words: **hoydenish** *adjective*, **hoydenism** *noun*.

hubris (HYOO-bris) *noun*, also given as **hybris** (HĪ-bris)

insolent pride or self-confidence; arrogance.

Related words: **hubristic** (hyoo-BRIS-tik) and **hybristic** (hī-BRIS-tik) *both adjectives*.

hyperbole (hī-PUR-bə-lee) *noun*

an exaggerated statement that is not meant to be taken literally.

Do not confuse **hyperbole** with **hyperbola** (hī-PUR-bə-lə), in geometry a plane curve of two equal infinite branches.

Related words: **hyperbolic** (HĪ-pər-BOL-ik) and **hyperbolical** *both adjectives*, **hyperbolically** *adverb*.

hypothecate (hī-POTH-ə-KAYT) *verb*

pledge or mortgage.

Related words: **hypothecation** (hī-POTH-ə-KAY-shən) and **hypothecator** (hī-POTH-ə-KAY-tər) *both nouns*.

I

iatrogenic (ī-A-trə-JEN-ik) *adjective*

of a disease or medical condition, caused by diagnosis or treatment by a physician.

Related word: **iatrogenicity** (ī-A-trə-jə-NIS-i-tee) *noun.*

iconoclast (ī-KON-ə-KLAST) *noun*

1. a person who attacks cherished beliefs.
2. a person who opposes the use of religious images in worship.

Related words: **iconoclasm** (ī-KON-ə-KLAZ-əm) *noun,* **iconoclastic** (ī-KON-ə-KLAS-tik) *adjective,* **iconoclastically** (ī-KON-ə-KLAS-ti-kə-lee) *adverb.*

idiosyncrasy (ID-ee-ə-SING-krə-see) *noun, plural* **idiosyncrasies**

a person's own attitude or way of thinking, behaving, etc. that is unlike that of any other.

Related words: **idiosyncratic** (ID-ee-oh-sin-KRAT-ik) *adjective,* **idiosyncratically** (ID-ee-oh-sin-KRAT-i-kə-lee) *adverb.*

ignominious (IG-nə-MIN-ee-əs) *adjective*

bringing contempt or disgrace; humiliating.

Related words: **ignominiously** *adverb,* **ignominiousness** and **ignominy** (IG-nə-MIN-ee) *both nouns.*

illusory (i-LOO-sə-ree) *adjective*

based on illusion; not real.

Related words: **illusorily** (i-LOO-sə-rə-lee) *adverb,* **illusoriness** (i-LOO-sə-ree-nis) *noun.*

immure (i-MYUUR) *verb*

1. imprison.
2. shut in; seclude.

Related words: **immurement** and **immuration** (IM-yə-RAY-shən) *both nouns.*

impalpable (im-PAL-pə-bəl) *adjective*

1. unable to be touched, intangible.
2. not easily grasped by the mind.

Related words: **impalpability** (im-PAL-pə-BIL-i-tee) *noun,* **impalpably** (im-PAL-pə-blee) *adverb.*

impassioned (im-PASH-ənd) *adjective*

full of deep feeling, passionate; ardent.

Related words: **impassionedly** *adverb,* **impassionedness** *noun.*

impassive (im-PAS-iv) *adjective*

not feeling or showing emotion; apathetic.

Related words: **impassively** *adverb,* **impassiveness** and **impassivity** (IM-pa-SIV-i-tee) *both nouns.*

impeach (im-PEECH) *verb*

1. call in question, discredit.
2. charge a public official before an appropriate tribunal with misconduct in office.

Do not use **impeach** to mean *convict a public official.* First one is **impeached**, meaning *charged,* then one may or may not be convicted.

Related words: **impeachable** (im-PEE-chə-bəl) *adjective,* **impeacher** and **impeachment** *both nouns.*

impecunious (IM-pi-KYOO-nee-əs) *adjective*

having little or no money; penniless, needy.

Related words: **impecuniously** *adverb,* **impecuniousness** and **impecuniosity** (IM-pi-KYOO-nee-OS-i-tee) *both nouns.*

imply (im-PLĪ) *verb*

1. suggest without stating directly; hint.
2. mean; signify.
3. involve necessarily.

Do not confuse **imply** with **infer**, which see.

importunate (im-POR-chə-nit) *adjective*
1. making persistent requests.
2. troublesome, annoying.

> Related words: **importunacy** (im-POR-chə-nə-see) and **importunateness** *both nouns*, **importunately** *adverb*, **importune** (IM-por-TOON) *verb*.

impracticable (im-PRAK-ti-kə-bəl) *adjective*
incapable of being put into practice.

> Do not confuse **impractable** with **impractical**, which means *unwise* or *not practical* and is used most often to denote unrealistic behavior in the management of one's finances. This distinction does not reflect the practice of permissive lexicographers, who bow to uninformed writers and speakers by treating **impracticable** and **impractical** as synonyms. A careful writer, however, preserves the differences in meaning of these two adjectives. You may find it helpful to realize that *unwise management of one's resources* may be termed **impractical**, while a foolish plan may be termed **impractable** because it *will never be put into practice*.

> Related words: **impracticability** (im-PRAK-ti-kə-BIL-i-tee) and **impracticableness** (im-PRAK-ti-kə-bəl-nis) *both nouns*, **impracticably** *adverb*.

imprecate (IM-prə-KAYT) *verb*
call down or invoke (a curse or evil) upon a person.

> Related words: **imprecation** (IM-pri-KAY-shən) and **imprecator** (IM-pri-KAY-tər) *both nouns*, **imprecatory** (IM-pri-kə-TOR-ee) *adjective*.

imprimatur (IM-pri-MAH-tər) *noun*
1. sanction or approval.
2. an official license to print, especially works sanctioned by the Catholic Church.

impudicity (IM-pyuu-DIS-i-tee) *noun*
shamelessness; immodesty.

impugn (im-PYOON) *verb*
1. express doubts about the truth or honesty of.

2. try to discredit (motives, etc.).

Related words: **impugnable** (im-PYOON-ə-bəl) *adjective*; **impugnability**, **impugner**, and **impugnment** *all nouns.*

inamorata (in-AM-ə-RAH-tə), **inamorato** (in-AM-ə-RAH-toh) *both nouns, plural* **inamoratas**, **inamoratos**
a lover; a sweetheart (*female* **inamorata**, *male* **inamorato**).

inanition (IN-ə-NISH-ən) *noun*
lack of vigor, especially exhaustion from lack of nourishment.

Do not confuse **inanition** with **inanity**, which see.

inanity (i-NAN-i-tee) *noun, plural* **inanities**
silliness; shallowness, superficiality.

When two words are similar in spelling, careless writers may think they share a meaning. So it is with **inanity**, which means *silliness*, and **inanition**, which means *lack of vigor*. These words are related in etymology, which accounts for their similarity in spelling, but have totally different meanings. Do not fall into the trap of confusing them. Try not to slip into **inanity** when you are exhausted or so hungry that you risk **inanition**.

Related words: **inane** (i-NAYN) *adjective*, **inanely** *adverb*.

inauspicious (IN-aw-SPISH-əs) *adjective*
1. not auspicious, ill-omened.
2. unlucky; unfavorable.

Related words: **inauspiciously** *adverb*, **inauspiciousness** *noun*.

inchoate (in-KOH-it) *adjective*
just begun; undeveloped.

Related words: **inchoately** *adverb*, **inchoateness** *noun*.

incredible (in-KRED-ə-bəl) *adjective*
unbelievable; hard to believe.

Do not confuse **incredible** with **incredulous**, which see.

Related words: **incredibility** (in-KRED-ə-BIL-i-tee) and **incredibleness** (in-KRED-ə-bəl-nis) *both nouns*, **incredibly** *adverb*.

incredulous (in-KREJ-ə-ləs) *adjective*
unbelieving; showing disbelief; skeptical.

When careless writers or speakers use **incredulous**, meaning *unbelieving*, in place of **incredible**, meaning *unbelievable*, they are guilty of an error that is becoming more and more common, particularly among ill-educated persons. No editor will let this boner pass, nor should you. Remember that you may appear **incredulous** when a high official of our national government shows **incredible** ignorance of how simple words are spelled.

Related words: **incredulity** (IN-kri-DOO-li-tee) and **incredulousness** (in-KREJ-ə-ləs-nis) *both nouns,* **incredulously** (in-KREJ-ə-ləs-lee) *adverb.*

incubus (IN-kyə-bəs) *noun, plural* **incubuses** and **incubi** (IN-kyə-BĪ)
1. a nightmare.
2. a person or thing that oppresses like a nightmare.
3. a spirit said to haunt or trouble sleeping people, especially by having sexual intercourse with sleeping women.

indefatigable (IN-di-FAT-i-gə-bəl) *adjective*
1. that cannot be tired out.
2. untiring, unwearying.

Related words: **indefatigability** (IN-di-FAT-i-gə-BIL-i-tee) and **indefatigableness** (IN-di-FAT-i-gə-bəl-nis) *both nouns,* **indefatigably** *adverb.*

indigenous (in-DIJ-ə-nəs) *adjective*
born or produced naturally in a country or region.

Related words: **indigenity** (IN-di-JEN-i-tee) and **indigenousness** (in-DIJ-ə-nəs-nis) *both nouns,* **indigenously** *adverb.*

indomitable (in-DOM-i-tə-bəl) *adjective*
1. having an unyielding spirit, unconquerable.
2. stubbornly persistent when faced with difficulty or opposition.

Related words: **indomitability** (in-DOM-i-tə-BIL-i-tee) and **indomitableness** (in-DOM-i-tə-bəl-nis) *both nouns,* **indomitably** *adverb.*

indurate (IN-duu-RAYT) *verb*
1. make or become hard.
2. make callous or unfeeling.
3. accustom or become accustomed.

Related words: **induration** (IN-duu-RAY-shən) *noun*, **indurative** (IN-duu-RAY-tiv) *adjective*.

inebriety (IN-i-BRĪ-i-tee) *noun*
drunkenness; the habit of drunkenness.

Related words: **inebriant** (in-EE-bree-ənt) and **inebriation** (in-EE-bree-AY-shən) *both nouns*, **inebriate** (in-EE-bree-it) and **inebriated** (in-EE-bree-AYT-id) *both adjectives*, **inebriate** (in-EE-bree-AYT) *verb*.

ineffable (in-EF-ə-bəl) *adjective*
too great to be described; inexpressible.

Related words: **ineffability** (in-EF-ə-BIL-i-tee) and **ineffableness** *both nouns*, **ineffably** *adverb*.

ineluctable (IN-i-LUK-tə-bəl) *adjective*
that cannot be avoided or overcome.

Related words: **ineluctability** (IN-i-LUK-tə-BIL-i-tee) *noun*, **ineluctably** *adverb*.

inexorable (in-EK-sər-ə-bəl) *adjective*
unable to be persuaded by request or entreaty; relentless.

Related words: **inexorability** (in-EK-sər-ə-BIL-i-tee) and **inexorableness** *both nouns*, **inexorably** *adverb*.

infamous (IN-fə-məs) *adjective*
See **notorious**.

infelicitous (IN-fə-LIS-i-təs) *adjective*
inappropriate; unfortunate; unhappy.

Related words: **infelicitously** *adverb*, **infelicity** *noun*.

infer (in-FUR) *verb*
reach an opinion from facts or reasoning.

Even though many people use **infer** and **imply** interchangeably, you should not fall into this practice, which obscures an important difference in meaning. **Imply** has as one of its meanings *hint or suggest without stating directly*, and the person performing such an action is actively hinting or suggesting. With **infer**, the person who is *reaching an opinion from facts or reasoning* is an interpreter of one's voice, facial expression, demeanor, etc.

An easy way to keep these two verbs distinct from one another is to remember that the sender of an unstated message is **implying**, and the receiver of the message is **inferring**.

Related words: **inference** (IN-fər-əns) *noun*, **inferential** (IN-fə-REN-shəl) *adjective*, **inferentially** *adverb*.

infrangible (in-FRAN-jə-bəl) *adjective*

1. unbreakable.
2. inviolable.

Related words: **infrangibility** (in-FRAN-jə-BIL-i-tee) and **infrangibleness** *both nouns*, **infrangibly** *adverb*.

ingenious (in-JEEN-yəs) *adjective*

1. clever at inventing new things or methods.
2. cleverly contrived.

Do not confuse **ingenious** with **ingenuous**, which see.

Related words: **ingeniously** *adverb*, **ingeniousness** and **ingenuity** (IN-jə-NOO-i-tee) *both nouns*.

ingenuous (in-JEN-yoo-əs) *adjective*

1. open, frank, sincere.
2. unsophisticated, naive.

The adjective **ingenuous** seems to have an attraction for ill-educated writers and speakers who are beguiled by the word's relative rareness compared with **ingenious**, a more common adjective they understand well. While **ingenuous** and **ingenious** a long time ago were synonyms, they now have entirely different meanings despite their similar spellings. Whatever the reason for the confusion of the two words, you must use them correctly. **Ingenuous** means *unsophisticated*, and **ingenious** means *clever at inventing*. **Ingenious** inventers who are **ingenuous**, therefore, will do well to hire a lawyer to protect their interests, lest they fail to protect themselves when dealing with possibly unscrupulous manufacturers interested in putting attractive inventions on the market.

Related words: **ingenuously** *adverb*, **ingenuousness** *noun*.

ingratiate (in-GRAY-shee-AYT) *verb*

bring (oneself) into a person's favor, especially in order to gain an advantage.

Related words: **ingratiating** and **ingratiatory** (in-GRAY-shee-ə-TOR-ee) *both adjectives*, **ingratiation** (in-GRAY-shee-AY-shən) *noun*.

innocuous (i-NOK-yoo-əs) *adjective*
1. not injurious, harmless.
2. insignificant and dull.

Related words: **innocuously** *adverb*, **innocuousness** and **innocuity** (IN-ə-KYOO-i-tee) *both nouns*.

inordinate (in-OR-də-nit) *adjective*
excessive; immoderate, intemperate.

Related words: **inordinately** *adverb*, **inordinateness** *noun*.

insatiate (in-SAY-shee-it) *adjective*
never satisfied.

Related words: **insatiately** *adverb*, **insatiateness** and **insatiety** (IN-sə-TĪ-ə-tee) *both nouns*.

inscrutable (in-SKROO-tə-bəl) *adjective*
1. impossible to understand or interpret.
2. mysterious, baffling.

Related words: **inscrutability** (in-SKROO-tə-BIL-i-tee) and **inscrutableness** (in-SKROO-tə-bəl-nis) *both nouns*, **inscrutably** *adverb*.

insensate (in-SEN-sayt) *adjective*
1. without physical sensation, unfeeling.
2. without good sense, foolish.

Related words: **insensately** *adverb*, **insensateness** *noun*.

instauration (IN-staw-RAY-shən) *noun*
restoration, renewal, renovation.

Related word: **instaurator** (IN-staw-RAY-tər) *noun*.

internecine (IN-tər-NEE-seen) *adjective*, also given as **internecive** (IN-tər-NEE-siv)
1. mutually destructive; deadly.
2. of a struggle within a nation, organization, or the like.

Sense 2 of **internecine** has given thoughtful writers and some lexicographers much to argue about. They prefer not to use this adjective in any sense but *mutually destructive or deadly*, as in

"The **internecine** war we waged in Europe in World War II," which clearly was not *a struggle within a nation*. But anyone who holds to this puristic view is bound to lose out. You are well advised to use the term in either of the senses given above and not argue against either sense. Notwithstanding, when you wish to use **internecine**, make sure the context indicates clearly which sense you intend.

intestate (in-TES-tayt) *adjective*
not having made a valid will before death occurs.

Related word: **intestacy** (in-TES-tə-see) *noun*.

intumesce (IN-tuu-MES) *verb*
swell up, become swollen.

Related words: **intumescence** (IN-tuu-MES-əns) *noun*, **intumescent** *adjective*.

inure (in-YUUR) *verb*
accustom, especially to something unpleasant; habituate.

Related word: **inuredness** (in-YUUR-id-nis) and **inurement**, *both nouns*.

inveigh (in-VAY) *verb*
attack violently or bitterly in words; revile.

Related word: **inveigher** *noun*.

inveterate (in-VET-ər-it) *adjective*
1. habitual.
2. firmly established.

Related words: **inveteracy** and **inveterateness** *both nouns*, **inveterately** *adverb*.

invidious (in-VID-ee-əs) *adjective*
1. likely to cause resentment because of real or imagined injustice.
2. hateful.

Related words: **invidiously** *adverb*, **invidiousness** *noun*.

irascible (i-RAS-ə-bəl) *adjective*
irritable, hot-tempered.

Related words: **irascibility** (i-RAS-ə-BIL-i-tee) and **irascibleness** *both nouns*, **irascibly** *adverb*.

irrefragable (i-REF-rə-gə-bəl) *adjective*
  indisputable, incontestable; unanswerable.

> Related words: **irrefragability** (i-REF-rə-gə-BIL-i-tee) and **irrefragableness** (i-REF-rə-gə-bəl-nis) *both nouns*, **irrefragably** (i-REF-rə-gə-blee) *adverb*.

isocracy (ī-SOK-rə-see) *noun, plural* **isocracies**
  a government in which all individuals have equal political power.

> Related words: **isocrat** (ī-sə-KRAT) *noun*, **isocratic** (ī-sə-KRAT-ik) *adjective*.

iterate (IT-ə-RAYT) *verb*
  utter again; repeat or perform again.

> Related words: **iteration** (IT-ə-RAY-shən) *noun*, **iterative** (IT-ər-ə-tiv) *adjective*, **iteratively** *adverb*.

J

jactation (jak-TAY-shən) *noun*
boasting; bragging.

janissary (JAN-ə-SER-ee) *noun, plural* **janissaries**; also given as **janizary** (JAN-ə-ZER-ee), *plural* **janizaries**
1. a devoted follower or supporter.
2. a Turkish soldier.
3. from the 14th to the 19th century, a member of the Turkish Sultan's guard.

jaundiced (JAWN-dist) *adjective*
1. discolored as if by jaundice (a disease marked by yellowness of the skin, of the whites of the eyes, etc.).
2. filled with resentment, envy, or jealousy.

jejune (ji-JOON) *adjective*
1. scanty.
2. meager, not nourishing.
3. unsatisfying to the mind; without significance; insipid.
4. puerile, childish; immature.
   Related words: **jejunely** *adverb*, **jejuneness** and **jejunity** (ji-JOON-ə-tee) *both nouns.*

jeremiad (JER-ə-MĪ-əd) *noun*
1. a prolonged mournful complaint about one's troubles.
2. a lamentation.

jerkin (JUR-kin) *noun*
a sleeveless jacket or vest.

jetsam (JET-səm) *noun*

goods thrown overboard from a ship in distress to lighten it, especially such goods that are washed ashore.

See **flotsam**.

jettison (JET-ə-sən) *verb*

1. throw (goods) overboard, especially to lighten a ship in distress.
2. discard (something that is no longer wanted); abandon.

Related word: **jettisonable** (JET-ə-sən-ə-bəl) *adjective*.

jocular (JOK-yə-lər) *adjective*

1. given to joking or jesting.
2. humorous; waggish.

Related words: **jocularity** (JOK-yə-LAR-i-tee) *noun*, **jocularly** (JOK-yə-lər-lee) *adverb*.

jocund (JOK-ənd) *adjective*

merry; cheerful; sprightly.

Related words: **jocundity** (joh-KUN-di-tee) *noun*, **jocundly** (JOK-ənd-lee) *adverb*.

jodhpurs (JOD-pərz) *noun*

riding breeches cut full about the hips and fitting closely from the knees to the ankles.

The aspect of **jodhpurs** that demands attention is its pronunciation, which is mistakenly and often heard as JOD-fərz. Take note of the correct pronunciation, JOD-pərz, and remember to pronounce **jodhpurs** correctly.

joust (jowst *or* joost, *also pronounced* just) *verb*

1. compete or struggle.
2. contend in a jousting tournament.

Related word: **jouster** *noun*.

justiciable (ju-STISH-ə-bəl) *adjective*

capable of being settled by the action of a court.

Related word: **justiciability** (ju-STISH-ə-BIL-i-tee) *noun*.

juxtapose (JUK-stə-POHZ) *verb*

place side by side or close together, especially for purposes of comparison or contrast.

Related word: **juxtaposition** (JUK-stə-pə-ZISH-ən) *noun*.

K

Kafkaesque (KAHF-kə-ESK) *adjective*

resembling, especially in nightmare quality, a state of affairs or a state of mind described by the writer Franz Kafka (1883–1924).

Related word: **Kafkaesquely** (KAHF-kə-ESK-lee) *adverb*.

kakemono (KAH-ke-MOH-noh) *noun, plural* **kakemonos** and **kakemono**

a Japanese wall-hanging, usually painted on paper or silk and mounted on rollers.

karma (KAHR-mə) *noun*

1. fate, destiny.
2. in Buddhism and Hinduism, the sum of a person's actions in one of his successive states of existence, seen as affecting the person's present life or his fate in the next incarnation.

Related word: **karmic** (KAHR-mik) *adjective*.

kedgeree (KEJ-ə-REE) *noun*

an East Indian dish made of rice, lentils, onions, eggs, etc.

kepi (KAY-pee) *noun, plural* **kepis**

a French military cap with a flat circular top and a visor.

kermis (KUR-mis) *noun*, also given as **kermess** and **kirmiss**, with the same pronunciations

1. in Holland and other Low Countries, an annual outdoor fair with much merrymaking.
2. a charity fair.

ketch (kech) *noun*

a small sailing vessel with foremast and mizzenmast.

kiosk (KEE-osk) *noun*

a light structure in a public place for use as a newsstand, refreshment stand, etc.

kismet (KIZ-mit) *noun*, also given as **kismat** (KIZ-mət)

fate; destiny.

kitsch (kich) *noun*

1. pretentiousness and lack of good taste in art.
2. an object of tawdry design.

Related word: **kitschy** *adjective*.

knout (nowt) *noun*

a flogging whip with a lash of leather thongs formerly used in Russia as an instrument of punishment.

Related word: **knout** *verb, punish with a knout.*

kyphosis (kī-FOH-sis) *noun*

an abnormal convex curvature of the spine.

Related word: **kyphotic** (kī-FOT-ik) *adjective*.

L

lachrymose (LAK-rə-MOHS) *adjective*

1. given to weeping.
2. tearful.

Related words: **lachrymosely** *adverb*, **lachrymosity** (LAK-rə-MOS-i-tee) *noun*.

laconic (lə-KON-ik) *adjective*

1. not talkative; terse;
2. concise.

Related words: **laconically** *adverb*, **laconicism** (lə-KON-ə-SIZ-əm) and **laconism** (LAK-ə-NIZ-əm) *both nouns*.

lacuna (lə-KYOO-nə) *noun, plural* **lacunae** (lə-KYOO-nee) *and* **lacunas**

1. a gap.
2. something missing from a book or argument etc.
3. a hiatus.

Related words: **lacunal** (lə-KYOON-əl), **lacunar** (lə-KYOO-nər), **lacunary** (lə-KYOON-ər-ee), and **lacunose** (lə-KYOO-nohs) *all adjectives*.

lambent (LAM-bənt) *adjective*

1. of light or flame, playing on a surface without burning it; with soft radiance.
2. of eyes, sky, etc., softly radiant.
3. of wit etc., dealing lightly and gracefully with a subject, lightly brilliant.

Related words: **lambency** (LAM-bən-see) *noun*, **lambently** *adverb*.

languid (LANG-gwid) *adjective*

lacking vigor or vitality; feeble, apathetic.

Related words: **languidly** *adverb*, **languidness** *noun*.

languorous (LANG-gər-əs) *adjective*

1. fatigued, lacking alertness; languid.
2. dull, listless, drooping.
3. of air, oppressively still.

Related words: **languorously** *adverb*, **languor** and **languorousness** *both nouns*.

lecher (LECH-ər) *noun*

1. a man given to unrestrained indulgence of sexual lust.
2. a lascivious man.

Related words: **lecherous** *adjective*, **lecherously** *adverb*, **lecherousness** and **lechery** (LECH-ə-ree) *both nouns*.

lectern (LEK-tərn) *noun*

a stand with a sloping top to hold a book or notes for a speaker or reader.

legerdemain (LEJ-ər-də-MAYN) *noun*

1. sleight of hand, magic tricks.
2. sophistry; trickery.

Related word: **legerdemainist** (LEJ-ər-də-MAYN-ist) *noun*.

lenity (LEN-i-tee) *noun, plural* **lenities**

1. gentleness; mercifulness.
2. an act of mercy.

Related word: **lenitive** *adjective*.

lese majesty (LEEZ MAJ-ə-stee), also given as **lèse-majesté** (les-mah-zhəs-TAY), as in French

1. an insult to a sovereign or ruler.
2. treason.
3. presumptuous behavior.

leviathan (lə-VĪ-ə-thən) *noun*

1. something of enormous size and power.
2. any huge sea creature.

libido (li-BEE-doh) *noun, plural* **libidos**

emotional energy or urge, especially that associated with sexual desire.

Related words: **libidinal** (li-BID-ə-nəl) and **libidinous** (li-BID-ən-əs) *both adjectives,* **libidinally** *adverb.*

limpid (LIM-pid) *adjective*

of a liquid, the atmosphere, or literary style, clear; lucid; transparent.

Related words: **limpidity** (lim-PID-i-tee) and **limpidness** (LIM-pid-nis) *both nouns,* **limpidly** *adverb.*

linchpin (LINCH-PIN) *noun,* also given as **lynchpin**

1. a person or thing that is vital to an organization, plan, etc.
2. a pin passed through the end of an axle to keep the wheel in position.

lissome (LIS-əm) *adjective,* also given as **lissom**

1. supple, flexible.
2. lithe, agile.

Related words: **lissomely** *adverb,* **lissomeness** *noun.*

littoral (LIT-ər-əl) *adjective*

1. of or pertaining to the shore.
2. *(noun)* the region lying along the shore.

loath (lohth) *adjective*

1. unwilling.
2. reluctant, disinclined.

Do not confuse **loath** with **loathe**, which see.

Related words: **loathly** *adverb,* **loathness** *noun.*

loathe (loh*th*) *verb*

feel great hatred and disgust for (a person or thing).

Loathe, meaning *feel great hatred,* and **loath**, meaning *reluctant,* are easily confused, first because of their similar spellings, secondly because many speakers pronounce both words as loh*th*. To avoid this confusion, you are well advised to pronounce **loath** as lohth. Save loh*th* for **loathe**, and remember that one should be eager to love and **loath** to **loathe**.

Related words: **loather** (LOHTH-ər) *noun*, **loathsome** (LOHTH-səm) *adjective*, **loathsomely** (LOHTH-səm-lee) *adverb*.

locum tenens (LOH-kəm TEN-inz), *plural* **locum tenentes** (LOH-kəm tə-NEN-teez)

a temporary substitute, especially for a physician or a member of the clergy.

Related word: **locum-tenency** (LOH-kəm-TEN-ən-see) *noun*.

logomachy (loh-GOM-ə-kee) *noun, plural* **logomachies**

1. a dispute about words.
2. a meaningless battle of words.

Related words: **logomachic** (LOH-gə-MAK-ik) and **logomachical** *both adjectives*, **logomachist** (loh-GOM-ə-kist) and **logomach** (LOH-gə-MAK) *both nouns*.

lordosis (lor-DOH-sis) *noun*

an abnormal forward curvature of the spine.

Related word: **lordotic** (lor-DOT-ik) *adjective*.

louche (loosh) *adjective*

1. shifty; shady.
2. disreputable.

lour (lowr) and **lower** (LOW-ər) *both verbs*

1. frown or scowl.
2. of the sky or clouds etc., look dark and threatening.

Related words: **lour** and **lower** *both nouns*, **loury** (LOW-ree) and **lowery** (LOW-ər-ee) *both adjectives*.

lubricious (loo-BRISH-əs) *adjective*

1. slippery; smooth.
2. oily.
3. lewd, salacious.

Related words: **lubricity** (loo-BRIS-i-tee) *noun*, **lubriciously** (loo-BRISH-əs-lee) *adverb*.

lucent (LOO-sənt) *adjective*

1. shining, luminous.
2. clear, translucent.

Related words: **lucency** *noun*, **lucently** *adverb*.

lucubration (LOO-kyuu-BRAY-shən) *noun*
1. laborious work, especially late at night.
2. a literary work, especially one of pedantic or elaborate character.

Related words: **lucubrate** (LOO-kyuu-BRAYT) *verb*, **lucubrator** (LOO-kyuu-BRAY-tər) *noun*, **lucubratory** (loo-KYOO-brə-TOR-ee) *adjective.*

Lucullan (loo-KUL-ən) *adjective*, also given as **Lucullean** and **Lucullian**, both pronounced LOO-kə-LEE-ən
marked by lavishness, especially said of feasting; sumptuous.

lugubrious (luu-GOO-bree-əs) *adjective*
dismal, mournful, gloomy, especially in an exaggerated manner.

Related words: **lugubriously** *adverb*, **lugubriousness** and **lugubriosity** (lə-GOO-bree-OS-i-tee) *both nouns.*

luxuriant (lug-ZHUUR-ee-ənt) *adjective*
growing profusely.

Do not confuse **luxuriant** with **luxurious**, which see.

Related words: **luxuriance** *noun*, **luxuriantly** *adverb.*

luxurious (lug-ZHUUR-ee-əs) *adjective*
1. supplied with luxuries.
2. very comfortable.

What a difference a change of suffixes makes! Many writers hesitate when having to make a choice between **luxurious** and **luxuriant**. While there is some argument over whether to accept these two adjectives as synonyms, you are best advised to take a hard line. Use **luxurious** in the sense of *supplied with luxuries* or *very comfortable*, and **luxuriant** in the sense of *growing profusely*, and you will be in excellent company, admired by editors and readers who appreciate careful usage. In short, you will be able to **luxuriate**, *enjoy yourself*, in the knowledge that your unimpeachable and carefully crafted prose style meets the highest standards.

Related words: **luxuriate** (lug-ZHUUR-ee-AYT) *verb*, **luxuriously** (lug-ZHUUR-ee-əs-lee) *adverb*, **luxuriousness** and **luxury** (LUG-zhə-ree) *both nouns.*

lycanthropy (lī-KAN-thrə-pee) *noun*

a delusion in which one imagines oneself to be a wild animal, especially a wolf, and exhibits depraved appetites.

Related words: **lycanthrope** (LĪ-kən-THROHP) *noun*, **lycanthropic** (LĪ-kən-THROP-ik) *adjective*.

M

macerate (MAS-ə-RAYT) *verb*

1. make or become soft by steeping in a liquid.
2. waste away by fasting.

Related words: **macerater** (MAS-ə-RAYT-ər), **macerator** and **maceration** (MAS-ə-RAY-shən) *all nouns*; **macerative** (MAS-ə-RAY-tiv) *adjective*.

maenad (MEE-nad) *noun*

1. a riotous or frenzied woman.
2. a Bacchante—a priestess of Bacchus—in classical mythology the god of wine.

magniloquent (mag-NIL-ə-kwənt) *adjective*

1. lofty in expression.
2. boastful; bombastic.
3. pompous.

Related words: **magniloquence** *noun*, **magniloquently** *adverb*.

maladroit (MAL-ə-DROYT) *adjective*

1. awkward, bungling.
2. tactless.

Related words: **maladroitly** *adverb*, **maladroitness** *noun*.

malediction (MAL-i-DIK-shən) *noun*

a curse.

Related words: **maledictive** (MAL-i-DIK-tiv) and **maledictory** (MAL-i-DIK-tə-ree) *both adjectives*.

malefic (mə-LEF-ik) *adjective*

of magical arts, harmful, malign, baneful.

Related words: **maleficent** (mə-LEF-ə-sənt) *adjective*, **maleficence** *noun*.

malevolent (mə-LEV-ə-lənt) *adjective*

1. wishing harm to others.
2. evil, injurious.

Related words: **malevolence** *noun*, **malevolently** *adverb*.

malinger (mə-LING-gər) *verb*

pretend to be ill in order to avoid work or shirk duty.

Related word: **malingerer** *noun*.

Mammon (MAM-ən) *noun*

wealth personified, regarded as an evil influence.

Related words: **mammonish** *adjective*, **mammonism** (MAM-ə-NIZ-əm) *noun*.

mansuetude (MAN-swi-TOOD) *noun*

meekness; gentleness.

marmoreal (mahr-MOR-ee-əl) *adjective*, also given as **marmorean** (mahr-MOR-ee-ən)

of or resembling marble.

Related word: **marmoreally** *adverb*.

martinet (MAHR-tə-NET) *noun*

1. a person who demands strict obedience.
2. a disciplinarian.

Related words: **martinetish** *adjective*, **martinetism** *noun*.

masticate (MAS-ti-KAYT) *verb*

chew (food).

Related words: **masticable** (MAS-ti-kə-bəl) and **masticatory** (MAS-ti-kə-TOR-ee) *both adjectives*, **mastication** (MAS-ti-KAY-shən) and **masticator** (MAS-ti-KAY-tər) *both nouns*.

matricide (MA-tri-SĪD) *noun*

1. a person who kills his mother.
2. the crime itself.

Related word: **matricidal** (MA-tri-SĪD-əl) *adjective*.

maudlin (MAWD-lin) *adjective*
sentimental in a silly or tearful way, especially from drunkenness.

> Related words: **maudlinism** and **maudlinness** *both nouns,* **maudlinly** *adverb.*

mawkish (MAW-kish) *adjective*
feebly or falsely sentimental.

> Related words: **mawkishly** *adverb,* **mawkishness** *noun.*

media (MEE-dee-ə) *plural noun, singular* **medium** (MEE-dee-əm)
the means of modern communication, especially the press, journals, radio, and television.

> Many words are mistreated in everyday speech, perhaps none more than **media** in the sense given above. **Media** is clearly a plural form of **medium** (which also has the plural **mediums** when used in some other senses, for example, in speaking of *persons who claim to be able to communicate with the spirits of dead persons*). So pervasive is the misuse of **media** as a singular noun—consider "The media is biased"—that it is regularly seen even in publications of high quality. Further, if you ever hear "The media are unbiased" in a news broadcast, you can bet that the item in which it appeared was written, edited, or spoken by a well-educated person, for example, an honors graduate of a leading university. In short, **media** as a singular noun is on the verge of winning the battle. At the same time, however, if you have the good fortune to write for learned readers, you will avoid criticism if you consistently use **media** as a plural noun, **medium** as a singular noun.

menarche (mə-NAHR-kee) *noun*
the onset of first menstruation.

> Related words: **menarcheal** (mə-NAHR-kee-əl) and **menarchial**, pronounced the same way, *both adjectives.*

mendacious (men-DAY-shəs) *adjective*
1. untruthful, telling lies, especially habitually.
2. false, untrue.

> Related words: **mendacity** (men-DAS-i-tee) and **mendaciousness** (men-DAY-shəs-nis) *both nouns,* **mendaciously** *adverb.*

menhir (MEN-heer) *noun*

a tall upright stone set in place in prehistoric times.

mephitic (mə-FIT-ik) *adjective*

1. of gases etc., smelling unpleasant.
2. poisonous.

Related words: **mephitically** *adverb*, **mephitis** (mə-FĪ-tis) *noun*.

mercurial (mər-KYUUR-ee-əl) *adjective*

1. liable to sudden changes of mood; flighty, fickle.
2. having a lively temperament; animated.

Related words: **mercuriality** (mər-KYUU-ree-AL-i-tee) and **mercurialness** (mər-KYUU-ree-əl-nis) *both nouns*, **mercurially** *adverb*.

meretricious (MER-i-TRISH-əs) *adjective*

showily attractive but cheap or insincere; tawdry.

Related words: **meretriciously** *adverb*, **meretriciousness** *noun*.

métier (MAY-tyay) *noun*

1. a person's trade, profession, or field of work.
2. a specialty, a forte.

mettle (MET-əl) *noun*

courage or strength of character.

Related word: **mettlesome** (MET-əl-səm) *adjective*.

miasma (mī-AZ-mə) *noun, plural* **miasmas** and **miasmata** (mī-AZ-mə-tə)

unpleasant or unwholesome air.

Related words: **miasmal**, **miasmatic** (MĪ-az-MAT-ik), **miasmatical** (MĪ-az-MAT-i-kəl), and **miasmic** (mī-AZ-mik) *all adjectives*.

micturition (MIK-chə-RISH-ən) *noun*

urination.

Related word: **micturate** (MIK-chə-RAYT) *verb*.

militate (MIL-i-TAYT) *verb*

1. have a substantial effect.
2. weigh heavily (in one's consideration).

Do not confuse **militate** with **mitigate**, which see.

Related word: **militation** (MIL-i-TAY-shən) *noun*.

mimesis (mi-MEE-sis) *noun*

imitation, mimicry.

> Related words: **mimetic** (mi-MET-ik) *adjective*, **mimetically** *adverb*.

minatory (MIN-ə-TOR-ee) *adjective*

threatening, menacing.

> Related word: **minatorily** (MIN-ə-TOR-i-lee) *adverb*.

misanthrope (MIS-ən-THROHP) *noun*

a person who dislikes people in general.

> Related words: **misanthropic** (MIS-ən-THROP-ik) and **misanthropical** *both adjectives*, **misanthropically** *adverb*, **misanthropy** (mis-AN-thrə-pee) *noun*.

miscegenation (mi-SEJ-ə-NAY-shən) *noun*

marriage or interbreeding of races, formerly said especially in the United States of whites with non-whites.

> Related word: **miscegenetic** (MIS-i-jə-NET-ik) *adjective*.

miscreant (MIS-kree-ənt) *noun*

1. a wrongdoer, a villain.

2. *(adjective)* depraved, villainous.

> Related word: **miscreancy** (MIS-kree-ən-see) *noun*.

misogamy (mi-SOG-ə-mee) *noun*

hatred of marriage.

> Related words: **misogamic** (MIS-ə-GAM-ik) *adjective*, **misogamist** (mi-SOG-ə-mist) *noun*.

misogyny (mi-SOJ-ə-nee) *noun*, also given as **misogynism** (mi-SOJ-ə-NIZ-əm)

hatred or mistrust of all women.

> Related word: **misogynist** *noun*.

misprision (mis-PRIZH-ən) *noun*

a wrong action or neglect by a public official.

mitigate (MIT-i-GAYT) *verb*

make less intense or serious or severe; appease.

> In recent years **mitigate** has been appearing incorrectly when **militate** is intended. **Militate** means *weigh heavily* and is used

correctly, for example, in "Only one factor **militated** against the success of our proposal." Remember that it is never correct to **mitigate** *against* anything; it is correct to **mitigate** anything if it is thought to be deserving of **mitigation**, as in "His contrite behavior *mitigated* our anger." Editors reject as incorrect the use of **mitigate** in place of **militate**, and you should too.

Related words: **mitigable** (MIT-i-gə-bəl), **mitigative** (MIT-i-GAY-tiv), and **mitigatory** (MIT-i-gə-TOR-ee) *all adjectives*; **mitigation** (MIT-i-GAY-shən) and **mitigator** (MIT-i-GAY-tər) *both nouns*.

moiety (MOY-i-tee) *noun, plural* **moieties**
1. approximately half of something.
2. a half.

monomania (MON-ə-MAY-nee-ə) *noun*
an obsession with one idea or interest.

Related words: **monomaniac** (MON-ə-MAY-nee-AK) *noun*, **monomaniacal** (MON-ə-mə-NĪ-ə-kəl) *adjective*

moot (moot) *adjective*
1. debatable, undecided.
2. doubtful.

Related word: **mootness** *noun*.

morass (mə-RAS) *noun*
1. something that confuses or impedes people; an entanglement.
2. a marsh, a bog.

mordant (MOR-dənt) *adjective*
characterized by a biting sarcasm.

Related words: **mordantly** *adverb*, **mordancy** (MOR-dən-see) *noun*.

morganatic (MOR-gə-NAT-ik) *adjective*
pertaining to a form of marriage between a man of high rank and a woman of lower rank who, along with their children, has no claim to the man's possessions or title.

Related word: **morganatically** *adverb*.

moribund (MOR-ə-BUND) *adjective*
1. in a dying state.

2. no longer effective.

Related words: **moribundity** (MOR-ə-BUN-di-tee) *noun,* **moribundly** (MOR-ə-BUND-lee) *adverb.*

motif (moh-TEEF) *noun*

1. a recurring design or feature in a literary or artistic work.
2. a short melody or theme that recurs and is developed in a piece of music.

mountebank (MOWN-tə-BANGK) *noun*

1. a swindler.
2. a charlatan.

Related word: **mountebankery** (MOWN-tə-BANGK-ə-ree) *noun.*

mucous (MYOO-kəs) *adjective*

1. of or like mucus.
2. secreting mucus.
3. covered with mucus.

Do not confuse **mucous** with **mucus**, which see.

Related word: **mucosity** (myoo-KOS-i-tee) *noun.*

mucus (MYOO-kəs) *noun*

the moist sticky substance that lubricates and forms a protective covering on the inner surfaces of the body's hollow organs.

The confusion of **mucus** and **mucous** can be understood readily. Not only are the two words spelled almost identically, but they are pronounced identically. Yet, no editors or writers worth their salt would fail to agree that **mucus** is a noun, and **mucous** is an adjective. So when they miss a confusion of the two words in a text they are working on, they are guilty of carelessness, not ignorance. Stay alert and avoid this boner.

mulct (mulkt) *verb*

take money away from (a person), as by a fine or taxation, or by dubious means.

muliebrity (MYOO-lee-EB-ri-tee) *noun*

1. womanhood.
2. normal characteristics of a woman.

Related word: **muliebral** (MYOO-lee-EB-rəl) *adjective.*

mutable (MYOO-tə-bəl) *adjective*

1. liable to change.
2. fickle, inconstant.

Related words: **mutability** (MYOO-tə-BIL-i-tee) and **mutableness** (MYOO-tə-bəl-nis) *both nouns,* **mutably** *adverb.*

myrmidon (MUR-mi-DON) *noun*

an unscrupulously faithful follower; a henchman.

N

nadir (NAY-dər) *noun*

1. the lowest point.
2. the time of greatest adversity.

Related word: **nadiral** (NAY-dər-əl) *adjective.*

narcissism (NAHR-sə-SIZ-əm) *noun*

1. a tendency to self-worship.
2. excessive or erotic interest in one's own personal features; vanity.

Related words: **narcissist** (NAHR-sə-sist) *noun,* **narcissistic** (NAHR-sə-SIS-tik) *adjective.*

nascent (NAY-sənt) *adjective*

1. in the act of being born.
2. just beginning to exist; immature.

Related word: **nascency** (NAY-sən-see) *noun.*

natter (NAT-ər) *verb*

1. chatter idly.
2. grumble.

Related word: **natter** *noun.*

nausea (NAW-zee-ə) *noun*

a feeling of sickness or extreme disgust.

See **nauseous**.

nauseate (NAW-zee-AYT) *verb*

cause to feel nausea.

See **nauseous**.

Related words: **nauseating** (NAW-zee-AY-ting) *adjective*, **nauseatingly** *adverb*.

nauseous (NAW-shəs) *adjective*
1. causing nausea.
2. experiencing nausea.

Some writers and editors insist stubbornly that **nauseous** should not be used in the second sense, *experiencing nausea*. Instead of "I feel nauseous," they prefer to write "I feel nauseated." Unfortunately for writers and editors so inclined, **nauseous** has been used in senses 1 and 2 for at least four centuries. Moreover, most people today use **nauseous** exclusively in sense 2, never thinking for a moment of speaking about **nauseous** medicines or **nauseous** anything else. So, whenever you feel sick to your stomach, ignore the advice of **nauseating**, self-proclaimed experts and express your feeling of **nausea** any way you wish. But first take something to restore you to good health.

Related words: **nauseously** *adverb*, **nauseousness** *noun*.

nebulous (NEB-yə-ləs) *adjective*
1. having no definite form.
2. indistinct.

Related words: **nebulously** *adverb*, **nebulousness** *noun*.

necrology (nə-KROL-ə-jee) *noun, plural* **necrologies**
1. a list of persons recently dead.
2. an obituary.

Related words: **necrological** (NEK-rə-LOJ-i-kəl) and **necrologic** (NEK-rə-LOJ-ik) *both adjectives*, **necrologically** (NEK-rə-LOJ-ə-klee) *adverb*, **necrologist** (nə-KROL-ə-jist) *noun*.

necropolis (nə-KROP-ə-lis) *noun, plural* **necropolises**
a cemetery, especially a cemetery of an ancient city.

Related word: **necropolitan** (NEK-rə-POL-i-tən) *adjective*.

nefarious (ni-FAIR-ee-əs) *adjective*
wicked.

Related words: **nefariously** *adverb*, **nefariousness** *noun*.

nemesis (NEM-ə-sis) *noun, plural* **nemeses** (NEM-ə-SEEZ)
1. retributive justice.
2. a downfall.
3. the agent of downfall.
4. a rival who is seen as inevitably victorious.

neologism (nee-OL-ə-JIZ-əm) *noun,* also given as **neology** (nee-OL-ə-jee)
1. a newly coined word or phrase.
2. the coining or using of new words.

Related words: **neologist** (nee-OL-ə-jist) *noun,* **neologistic** (nee-OL-ə-JIS-tik) and **neologistical** (nee-OL-ə-JIS-ti-kəl) *both adjectives,* **neologize** (nee-OL-ə-JĪZ) *verb.*

neonatal (NEE-oh-NAYT-əl) *adjective*
of or relating to a newborn child.

Related word: **neonatally** *adverb.*

neonate (NEE-ə-NAYT) *noun*
1. a newborn child.
2. a child in its first 28 days.

neoteric (NEE-ə-TER-ik) *adjective*
1. modern, recent.
2. newfangled.

Related word: **neoterically** *adverb.*

nepotism (NEP-ə-TIZ-əm) *noun*
favoritism shown to relatives in appointing them to jobs.

Related words: **nepotist** (NEP-ə-tist) *noun,* **nepotistic** (NEP-ə-TIS-tik) and **nepotistical** *both adjectives.*

nescience (NESH-əns) *noun*
1. absence of knowledge.
2. ignorance.

Related word: **nescient** *adjective.*

nevus (NEE-vəs) *noun, plural* **nevi** (NEE-vī)
a birthmark consisting of a mole or a red patch on the skin.

Related word: **nevoid** (NEE-void) *adjective.*

nexus (NEK-səs) *noun, plural* **nexuses** or **nexus**
a bond, link, or connection.

nirvana (nir-VAH-nə) *noun*
in Buddhist and Hindu teaching, the state of perfect bliss attained when the soul is freed from all suffering and absorbed into the supreme spirit.

Related word: **nirvanic** *adjective*.

noctambulist (nok-TAM-byə-list) *noun*, also given as **noctambule** (nok-TAM-byool)
a sleepwalker; a somnambulist.

Related words: **noctambulant** (nok-TAM-byə-lənt), **noctambulistic** (nok-TAM-byə-LIS-tik), and **noctambulous** (nok-TAM-byə-ləs) *all adjectives*; **noctambulism** (nok-TAM-byə-LIZ-əm) and **noctambulation** (nok-TAM-byə-LAY-shən) *both nouns*.

nocuous (NOK-yoo-əs) *adjective*
1. harmful, likely to cause damage.
2. noxious.

Related words: **nocuously** *adverb*, **nocuousness** *noun*.

noisome (NOY-səm) *adjective*
1. harmful.
2. offensive, disgusting.
3. noxious.

Obviously, **noisome** shares no meaning with **noise** or **noisy**, yet careless writers mistakenly use this adjective as a synonym for **noisy**. Remember that while **noisy** environments may be thought of as **noisome**, it is because they are often considered to be *harmful* or *offensive*. The two adjectives are not even remotely synonymous.

Related words: **noisomely** *adverb*, **noisomeness** *noun*.

nonpareil (NON-pə-REEL) *adjective*
1. without equal; peerless.
2. *(noun)* a person having no equal.
3. *(noun)* a chocolate candy decorated with sugar pellets.

nostrum (NOS-trəm) *noun*
1. a quack remedy.

2. a patent medicine.

3. a panacea.

notorious (noh-TOR-ee-əs) *adjective*
well known, especially in an unfavorable way.

> Many writers and speakers mistakenly use **famous** as an exact synonym for **notorious**, which is better thought of as a close synonym for **infamous**. Save **famous** for persons of enviable achievements and good reputations. **Infamous** persons are those having or deserving very bad reputations.

> Related words: **notoriously** *adverb*, **notoriousness** and **notoriety** (NOH-tə-RĪ-i-tee) *both nouns*.

noxious (NOK-shəs) *adjective*

1. unpleasant; injurious to health.

2. corrupting, morally harmful; pernicious.

3. nocuous.

> Related words: **noxiously** *adverb*, **noxiousness** *noun*.

nugatory (NOO-gə-TOR-ee) *adjective*

1. trifling, worthless; futile.

2. inoperative, ineffective, not valid.

nyctalopia (NIK-təl-OH-pee-ə) *noun*
night blindness.

> Related word: **nyctalopic** (NIK-təl-OP-ik) *adjective*.

0

obdurate (OB-duu-rit) *adjective*

1. stubborn, unyielding.
2. impenitent.

    Related words: **obduracy** (OB-duu-rə-see) and **obdurateness** (OB-duu-rit-nis) *both nouns*, **obdurately** *adverb*.

obeisance (oh-BAY-səns) *noun*

1. deference or homage.
2. a deep bow or curtsy.

    Related words: **obeisant** *adjective*, **obeisantly** *adverb*.

objurgate (OB-jər-GAYT) *verb*

denounce, upbraid harshly; revile.

    Related words: **objurgation** (OB-jər-GAY-shən) and **objurgator** (OB-jər-GAY-tər) *both nouns*, **objurgative** (əb-JUR-gə-tiv) and **objurgatory** (əb-JUR-gə-TOR-ee) *both adjectives*, **objurgatively** (əb-JUR-gə-tiv-lee) and **objurgatorily** (əb-JUR-gə-TOR-ə-lee) *both adverbs*.

obloquy (OB-lə-kwee) *noun, plural* **obloquies**

1. verbal censure or abuse; detraction.
2. discredit, disgrace, or bad reputation as a result of being badly spoken of.

obnubilate (ob-NOO-bə-LAYT) *verb*

cloud over; darken; obscure.

    Related word: **obnubilation** (ob-NOO-bə-LAY-shən) *noun*.

obsecrate (OB-si-KRAYT) *verb*
1. plead, beseech.
2. supplicate in the name of something sacred.

> Related word: **obsecration** (OB-si-KRAY-shən) *noun*.

obsequies (OB-si-kweez) *plural noun, singular* **obsequy**
funeral rites; a funeral.

obsequious (əb-SEE-kwee-əs) *adjective*
obsessively or sickeningly respectful.

> Related words: **obsequiously** *adverb*, **obsequiousness** *noun*.

obtrude (əb-TROOD) *verb*
1. force (oneself or one's ideas) on others.
2. thrust forth; push out.

> Related words: **obtruder** and **obtrusion** (əb-TROO-zhən) *both nouns*, **obtrusive** (əb-TROO-siv) *adjective*, **obtrusively** *adverb*.

obviate (OB-vee-AYT) *verb*
1. make unnecessary.
2. neutralize (inconvenience, danger, etc.).

occlude (ə-KLOOD) *verb*
1. close, obstruct, stop up.
2. shut in.

> Related words: **occludent** *adjective*, **occluder** and **occlusion** (ə-KLOO-zhən) *both nouns*.

ochlocracy (ok-LOK-rə-see) *noun*
mob rule.

> Related words: **ochlocrat** (OK-lə-KRAT) *noun*, **ochlocratic** (OK-lə-KRAT-ik) and **ochlocratical** (OK-lə-KRAT-ə-kəl) *both adjectives*, **ochlocratically** *adverb*.

odalisque (OHD-əl-isk) *noun*, also given as **odalisk**
a female slave or concubine, especially in a harem.

odious (OH-dee-əs) *adjective*
hateful, detestable; disgusting, offensive, repugnant.

> **Odious**, influenced by its superficial resemblance to **odorous**, is frequently used mistakenly with the meaning of *ill-smelling*.

Speakers and writers who make this mistake open themselves to ridicule. Take care.

Related words: **odiously** *adverb*, **odiousness** *noun*.

oenophile (EE-nə-FĪL) *noun*
a lover of wine, especially a wine connoisseur.

Related words: **oenophilia** (EE-nə-FIL-ee-ə) *noun*, **oenophilic** (EE-nə-FIL-ik) *adjective*.

offal (AW-fəl) *noun*
1. the parts cut off as waste from a butchered animal.
2. carrion.
3. refuse or waste in general; dregs.

officious (ə-FISH-əs) *adjective*
aggressively asserting one's authority; bossy.

Do not confuse **officious** with the well-known word **official**, even though some **officials** may be **officious**.

Related words: **officiously** *adverb*, **officiousness** *noun*.

oligarchy (OL-i-GAHR-kee) *noun, plural* **oligarchies**
1. a form of government in which power is in the hands of a few people.
2. the group that holds this power.
3. a country governed this way.

Related words: **oligarch** (OL-i-GAHRK) *noun*, **oligarchic** (OL-i-GAHR-kik) and **oligarchical** *both adjectives*, **oligarchically** *adverb*.

operose (OP-ə-ROHS) *adjective*
1. of work, requiring much effort; tedious, laborious.
2. of a person, industrious.

Related words: **operosely** *adverb*, **operoseness** *noun*.

opprobrious (ə-PROH-bree-əs) *adjective*
1. of words etc., showing scorn or reproach.
2. abusive, vituperative.

Related words: **opprobriously** *adverb*, **opprobriousness** and **opprobrium** (ə-PROH-bree-əm) *both nouns*.

ordure (OR-jər) *noun*

manure, dung, excrement.

> Related word: **ordurous** (OR-jər-əs) *adjective*.

orison (OR-ə-zən) *noun*

a prayer.

orotund (OR-ə-TUND) *adjective*

1. with full voice, imposing, dignified.
2. pompous, pretentious.

> Do not confuse **orotund** with **rotund**, which see.
>
> Related word: **orotundity** (OR-ə-TUN-di-tee) *noun*.

orthoepy (or-THOH-ə-pee) *noun*

the study of correct pronunciation.

> Related words: **orthoepic** (OR-thoh-EP-ik), **orthoepical**, and **orthoepistic** (OR-thoh-ə-PIS-tik) *all adjectives*; **orthoepist** (or-THOH-ə-pist) *noun*.

orthography (or-THOG-rə-fee) *noun, plural* **orthographies**

1. correct or conventional spelling.
2. a perspective projection used in maps or elevations.

> Related words: **orthographer** (or-THOG-rə-fər) *noun*, **orthographic** (OR-thə-GRAF-ik) and **orthographical** *both adjectives*, **orthographically** *adverb*.

oscitation (os-i-TAY-shən) *noun*

1. yawning.
2. drowsiness.

> Related words: **oscitant** (OS-i-tənt) *adjective*, **oscitance** and **oscitancy** *both nouns*.

ostensible (o-STEN-sə-bəl) *adjective*

1. pretended.
2. professed.
3. put forward as actual or genuine to conceal the real.

> Related word: **ostensibly** (o-STEN-sə-blee) *adverb*.

otiose (OH-shee-OHS) *adjective*

not required, serving no practical purpose; superfluous.

Related words: **otiosely** *adverb*, **otioseness** and **otiosity** (OH-shee-OS-i-tee) *both nouns.*

outré (oo-TRAY) *adjective*

outside the bounds of what is considered correct or proper.

overweening (OH-vər-WEE-ning) *adjective*

1. arrogant, conceited, presumptuous.
2. overconfident.
3. excessive.

Related words: **overweeningly** *adverb*, **overweeningness** *noun.*

oviparous (oh-VIP-ər-əs) *adjective*

producing young by means of eggs expelled from the body before they are hatched.

Related words: **oviparity** (oh-və-PAR-i-tee) and **oviparousness** (oh-VIP-ər-əs-nis) *both nouns,* **oviparously** *adverb.*

oxymoron (OK-si-MOR-on) *noun*

a figure of speech combining seemingly contradictory expressions.

Related word: **oxymoronic** (OK-see-mə-RON-ik) *adjective.*

P

palindrome (PAL-in-DROHM) *noun*

a word or phrase that reads the same backward as forward.

> Related words: **palindromic** (PAL-in-DROM-ik) and **palindromical** *both adjectives*, **palindromically** *adverb*, **palindromist** (pə-LIN-droh-mist) *noun*.

palliative (PAL-ee-ə-tiv) *adjective*

1. reducing the bad effects of something.
2. *(noun)* something that does this.

> Related word: **palliatively** *adverb*.

pallid (PAL-id) *adjective*

pale, especially from illness.

> Related words: **pallidly** *adverb*, **pallidness** *noun*.

palmy (PAH-mee) *adjective*

1. flourishing, prosperous.
2. triumphant.

palpable (PAL-pə-bəl) *adjective*

1. able to be touched or felt.
2. easily perceived; obvious.

> Related words: **palpability** (PAL-pə-BIL-i-tee) and **palpableness** (PAL-pə-bəl-nis) *both nouns*, **palpably** (PAL-pə-blee) *adverb*.

panacea (PAN-ə-SEE-ə) *noun*

a remedy for all kinds of diseases or troubles.

> Related word: **panacean** (PAN-ə-SEE-ən) *adjective*.

panache (pə-NASH) *noun*
1. a grand or flamboyant manner.
2. swagger, verve.

pandemic (pan-DEM-ik) *adjective*
1. of a disease, occurring over a whole country or the whole world.
2. *(noun)* such a disease.

Related word: **pandemicity** (PAN-də-MIS-i-tee) *noun*.

panegyric (PAN-i-JĪR-ik) *noun*
a speech or piece of writing praising a person or thing; a tribute.

Related words: **panegyrical** *adjective*, **panegyrically** *adverb*, **panegyrist** (PAN-i-JĪR-ist) *noun*, **panegyrize** (PAN-i-jə-RĪZ) *verb*.

panjandrum (pan-JAN-drəm) *noun*
1. a mock title of a self-important personage.
2. a pompous official or pretender.

paraclete (PAR-ə-KLEET) *noun*
an advocate, especially a person who intercedes on behalf of someone.

paradigm (PAR-ə-DĪM) *noun*
1. something serving as an example or model of how things should be done.
2. in grammar, a set of forms of the inflection of a noun, a verb, etc.

Related words: **paradigmatic** (PAR-ə-dig-MAT-ik) and **paradigmatical** *both adjectives*, **paradigmatically** *adverb*.

parameter (pə-RAM-i-tər) *noun*
1. a variable quantity or quality that restricts or gives a particular form to the thing it characterizes.
2. a boundary, a limit.

Whereas **parameter** formerly was primarily a scholarly word, used only in sense 1 above, recent years have seen its meaning extended in popular use to sense 2. Perhaps because **parameter** has a cachet lacking in *boundary* or *limit*, this once-rare word has rapidly become the word of choice for many speakers and writers, who use it only in sense 2 and appear entirely unaware of **parameter** in sense 1. Even educated persons use it in sense 2, but as a careful writer you will do well to use **parameter** exclusively in sense 1, for example, "Height and weight were the parameters of immediate interest to us." When writing of boundaries or limits, use *boundary* or *limit*, two straightforward and simple words that everyone will readily understand.

Related words: **parametric** (PAR-ə-MET-rik) and **parametrical** *both adjectives*.

paronomasia (PAR-ə-noh-MAY-zhə) *noun*

1. word play; punning.
2. a pun.

Related words: **paronomastic** (PAR-ə-noh-MAS-tik) *adjective*, **paronomastically** *adverb*.

parricide (PAR-ə-SĪD) *noun*

1. the act of killing one's father, mother, or other close relative.
2. a person who commits parricide.

Do not confuse **parricide** with **patricide**, which see.

Related word: **parricidal** (PAR-ə-SĪD-əl) *adjective*.

parsimony (PAHR-sə-MOH-nee) *noun*

carefulness in use of money etc., especially excessive carefulness with money; stinginess.

Related words: **parsimonious** (PAHR-sə-MOH-nee-əs) *adjective*, **parsimoniously** *adverb*, **parsimoniousness** *noun*.

parturition (PAHR-tuu-RISH-ən) *noun*

1. the process of giving birth.
2. childbirth.

pastiche (pa-STEESH) *noun*

a musical or other composition made up of selections from various sources; a medley.

pathos (PAY-thos) *noun*

in literature, speech, etc., a quality that arouses pity or sadness.

patricide (PA-trə-SĪD) *noun*

1. the act of killing one's father.
2. a person who commits patricide.

Do not confuse **patricide** with **parricide**. A **parricide** is taken to mean a person who may kill close relatives, not just his father.

Related word: **patricidal** (PA-trə-SĪD-əl) *adjective*.

patronize (PAY-trə-nīz) *verb*
1. be a regular customer at (a store etc.).
2. treat (someone) in a condescending manner.

Related words: **patronizable** (PAY-trə-Nī-zə-bəl) and **patronizing** (PAY-trə-Nī-zing) *both adjectives*, **patronization** (PAY-trən-i-ZAY-shən) and **patronizer** (PAY-trə-NĪZ-ər) *both nouns*.

patronymic (PA-trə-NIM-ik) *noun*, also given as **patronym** (PA-trə-nim)
1. a name derived from the name of a father or ancestor.
2. a family name.

patulous (PACH-ə-ləs) *adjective*
1. open; gaping.
2. expanded.
3. of a tree or tree limbs, spreading.

Related words: **patulously** *adverb*, **patulousness** *noun*.

peccable (PEK-ə-bəl) *adjective*
1. liable to sin or error.
2. capable of sinning.

Do not confuse **peccable** with **peccant**, which see.

Related word: **peccability** (PEK-ə-BIL-i-tee) *noun*.

peccadillo (PEK-ə-DIL-oh) *noun*, *plural* **peccadilloes** and **peccadillos**
a trivial sin or offense.

peccant (PEK-ənt) *adjective*
1. guilty of a moral offense.
2. sinning; offending.

Keep the distinction between **peccable**, meaning *capable of sinning*, and **peccant**, meaning *guilty of a moral offense*. While one may argue that everyone is **peccable**, we hope that not everyone is **peccant**.

Related words: **peccancy** and **peccantness** *both nouns*, **peccantly** *adverb*.

peculation (PEK-yə-LAY-shən) *noun*
embezzlement.

Related words: **peculate** (PEK-yə-LAYT) *verb*, **peculator** (PEK-yə-LAY-tər) *noun*.

pederasty (PED-ə-RAS-tee) *noun*
an act of sodomy committed by men, especially by men with boys.

Related words: **pederast** (PED-ə-RAST) *noun*, **pederastic** (PED-ə-RAS-tik) *adjective*, **pederastically** *adverb*.

pejorative (pi-JOR-ə-tiv) *adjective*
disparaging; derogatory.

Related words: **pejorative** *noun*, **pejoratively** *adverb*.

pellucid (pə-LOO-sid) *adjective*
1. very clear in expression.
2. transparent; translucent.

Related words: **pellucidity** (PEL-uu-SID-i-tee) and **pellucidness** (pə-LOO-sid-nis) *both nouns*, **pellucidly** (pə-LOO-sid-lee) *adverb*.

penchant (PEN-chənt *or* pahn-SHAHN) *noun*
a liking or inclination.

penultimate (pi-NUL-tə-mit) *adjective*
next to last.

percipient (pər-SIP-ee-ənt) *adjective*
1. capable of perceiving.
2. showing keenness of insight; discerning.

Related words: **percipience** and **percipiency** *both nouns*.

perdurable (pər-DUUR-ə-bəl) *adjective*
1. very durable.
2. permanent, eternal.

Related words: **perdurability** (pər-DUUR-ə-BIL-i-tee) and **perdurableness** (pər-DUUR-ə-bəl-nis) *both nouns*, **perdurably** (pər-DUUR-ə-blee) *adverb*, **perdure** (pər-DUUR) *verb*.

peregrination (PER-i-grə-NAY-shən) *noun*
1. traveling.
2. a journey.

Related words: **peregrinate** (PER-i-grə-NAYT) *verb*, **peregrinator** (PER-i-grə-NAY-tər) *noun*.

perfidious (pər-FID-ee-əs) *adjective*
1. treacherous, disloyal.
2. deceitful.

Related words: **perfidiously** *adverb*, **perfidiousness** and **perfidy** (PUR-fi-dee) *both nouns*.

peripatetic (PER-ə-pə-TET-ik) *adjective*
going from place to place; itinerant.

Related words: **peripatetically** *adverb*, **peripateticism** (PER-ə-pə-TET-ə-SIZ-əm) *noun*.

periphrasis (pə-RIF-rə-sis) *noun*, *plural* **periphrases** (pə-RIF-rə-SEEZ)
a roundabout phrase or way of speaking; a circumlocution.

Related word: **periphrastic** (PER-ə-FRAS-tik) *adjective*, **periphrastically** *adverb*.

pernicious (pər-NISH-əs) *adjective*
having a very harmful effect; ruinous.

Related words: **perniciously** *adverb*, **perniciousness** *noun*.

perquisite (PUR-kwə-zit) *noun*
a profit, allowance, privilege, etc. given or looked upon as one's right in addition to wages or salary.

perseverate (pər-SEV-ə-RAYT) *verb*
repeat something insistently or over and over again.

Related words: **perseveration** (pər-SEV-ə-RAY-shən) *noun*, **perseverative** (pər-SEV-ə-RAY-tiv) *adjective*.

persiflage (PUR-sə-FLAHZH) *noun*
1. banter.
2. a flippant way of treating a subject.

personify (pər-SON-ə-FĪ) *verb*
1. represent (an idea) in human form or (a thing) as having human characteristics.
2. embody (a quality) in one's life or behavior.

Related words: **personifiable** (pər-SON-i-FĪ-ə-bəl) *adjective*, **personification** (pər-SON-ə-fi-KAY-shən) and **personifier** (pər-SON-ə-FĪ-ər) *both nouns*.

perspicacious (PUR-spi-KAY-shəs) *adjective*
having or showing great insight; discerning.

> Do not confuse **perspicacious** with **perspicuous**, which see.

> Related words: **perspicacity** (PUR-spi-KAS-i-tee) and **perspicaciousness** *both nouns,* **perspicaciously** *adverb.*

perspicuous (pər-SPIK-yoo-əs) *adjective*
1. clearly expressed; easily understood, lucid.
2. of a person, expressing things clearly.

> Permissive lexicographers, always eager to reflect common usage, may show **perspicuous** as a synonym for **perspicacious**, thereby encouraging writers to misuse the two words. While these adjectives have long been confused by the unwary, perhaps because their spellings are so similar, **perspicuous** and **perspicacious** have different meanings, and careful writers and editors are able to keep them apart. If you wish to use one of these adjectives to describe a person *who expresses things clearly,* choose **perspicuous**. Again, if you wish to characterize a piece of writing or an explanation as *lucid,* choose **perspicuous**. On the other hand, if you wish to characterize a person, a person's thoughts, or a piece of writing or an explanation as *having or showing great insight,* choose **perspicacious**. Show your **perspicacity** by thinking and writing **perspicuously**.

> Related words: **perspicuity** (PUR-spi-KYOO-i-tee) and **perspicuousness** (pər-SPIK-yoo-əs-nis) *both nouns,* **perspicuously** *adverb.*

pertinacious (PUR-tə-NAY-shəs) *adjective*
1. holding firmly to an opinion or course of action.
2. persistent and determined; resolute.
3. obstinate.

> Related words: **pertinacity** (PUR-tə-NAS-i-tee) and **pertinaciousness** (PUR-tə-NAY-shəs-nis) *both nouns,* **pertinaciously** *adverb.*

petard (pi-TAHRD) *noun*
a small bombshell formerly used to blow in a castle door, breach a wall, etc.

pettifog (PET-ee-FOG) *verb*
1. quibble.

2. engage in legal trickery.

Related words: **pettifogger** and **pettifoggery** *both nouns*, **pettifogging** *adjective*.

petulance (PECH-ə-ləns) *noun*
unreasonable impatience; peevishness.

Related words: **petulant** (PECH-ə-lənt) *adjective*, **petulantly** *adverb*.

piacular (pī-AK-yə-lər) *adjective*
1. sinful, wicked.
2. culpable; requiring atonement.
3. atoning, expiatory.

Related words: **piacularly** *adverb*, **piacularness** *noun*.

picaresque (PIK-ə-RESK) *adjective*
of fiction, dealing with the adventures of a rogue.

picayune (PIK-ə-YOON) *adjective*, also given as **picayunish** (PIK-ə-YOON-ish)
1. trifling, petty.
2. mean, contemptible.

Related words: **picayunishly** *adverb*, **picayunishness** *noun*.

pilose (PĪ-lohs) *adjective*, also given as **pilous** (PĪ-ləs)
covered with hair, especially soft hair; hairy.

Related word: **pilosity** (pī-LOS-i-tee) *noun*.

pinguid (PING-gwid) *adjective*
1. fat.
2. oily; greasy.

Related word: **pinguidity** (ping-GWID-i-tee) *noun*.

piscivorous (pi-SIV-ər-əs) *adjective*
fish-eating.

placebo (plə-SEE-boh) *noun, plural* **placebos** or **placeboes** (plə-SEE-bohz)
a harmless substance given as if it were medicine, to humor a patient or as a dummy pill etc. in a controlled experiment.

plangent (PLAN-jənt) *adjective*
1. of sounds, loud and reverberating.

2. of sounds, mournful.

Related words: **plangency** *noun,* **plangently** *adverb.*

platitude (PLAT-i-TOOD) *noun*
a commonplace remark, especially one uttered solemnly as if it were new.

Related words: **platitudinal** (PLAT-i-TOOD-ən-əl) and **platitudinous** *both adjectives,* **platitudinarian** (PLAT-i-TOOD-ən-AIR-ee-ən) *noun,* **platitudinize** (PLAT-i-TOOD-ən-īz) *verb.*

plenitude (PLEN-i-TOOD) *noun*
abundance; profusion.

A common error in speech is to pronounce this word as though it were written *plentitude.* An understandable error, but strictly a no-no. Like saying *irregardless* rather than *regardless.*

Related word: **plenitudinous** (PLEN-i-TOOD-ə-nəs) *adjective.*

pleonasm (PLEE-ə-NAZ-əm) *noun*
an expression in which a word or words are redundant.

Related words: **pleonastic** (PLEE-ə-NAS-tik) *adjective,* **pleonastically** (PLEE-ə-NAS-ti-kə-lee) *adverb.*

plethora (PLETH-ər-ə) *noun*
an overabundance; an excess amount.

Related words: **plethoric** (ple-THOR-ik) *adjective,* **plethorically** (ple-THOR-i-kə-lee) *adverb.*

poetaster (POH-it-AS-tər) *noun*
an inferior poet.

Related words: **poetastering, poetasterism,** and **poetastry** *all nouns;* **poetastric** (POH-it-AS-trik) and **poetastrical** (POH-it-AS-tri-kəl) *both adjectives.*

polyhistor (POL-ee-HIS-tər) and **polymath** (POL-ee-MATH) *both nouns*
1. a person with knowledge of many subjects.
2. a great scholar.

Related words: **polyhistoric** (POL-ee-hi-STOR-ik) *adjective,* **polyhistorian** (POL-ee-hi-STOR-ee-ən) and **polyhistory** *both nouns;* **polymath** and **polymathic** (POL-ee-MATH-ik) *both adjectives,* **polymathy** (pə-LIM-ə-thee) *noun.*

popinjay (POP-in-JAY) *noun*
a conceited and talkative person.

posit (POZ-it) *verb*
state or assume as fact.

postprandial (pohst-PRAN-dee-əl) *adjective*
after a meal, especially dinner.

Related word: **postprandially** *adverb*.

practicable (PRAK-ti-kə-bəl) *adjective*
1. able to be put into practice.
2. usable; feasible.

Do not confuse **practicable** with **practical**, which see.

Related words: **practicability** (PRAK-ti-kə-BIL-i-tee) and **practicableness** (PRAK-ti-kə-bəl-nis) *both nouns*, **practicably** (PRAK-ti-kə-blee) *adverb*.

practical (PRAK-ti-kəl) *adjective*
1. involving activity as distinct from study or theory.
2. capable of being put to use; useful.
3. of people, clever at doing and making things.
4. virtual.

Writers and speakers, perhaps seduced by the fatal charm of an adjective less common compared with the perceived banality of an adjective encountered more often, slip into the trap of using **practicable** when they would be well advised to use **practical**. By doing so, they blur the important distinction between that which is *usable*, **practicable**, and that which is *useful*, **practical**. This happens particularly when writers and speakers are discussing plans, ideas, or the like. Thus, when they wish to say something is *useful*, the adjective of choice should be **practical**, perhaps ignoring the question of whether it can be accomplished. When, however, writers and speakers wish to say something is *feasible* or *usable*, that is, *able to be put into practice*, the adjective of choice should be **practicable**. Many things, many improvements, and the like may be said to be useful—**practical**—but how many useful ideas are also feasible—**practicable**? In trying to use the two adjectives correctly in your own writing and speech, it may be helpful to remember that many practical, *useful*, inventions may never see the light of day because they are not **practicable**, *feasible* or *usable*. In addition, many people may be characterized as **practical**, *clever at doing or making things*, but never as **practicable**.

Related words: **practicality** (PRAK-ti-KAL-i-tee) and **practicalness** (PRAK-ti-kəl-nis) *both nouns*, **practically** (PRAK-ti-kə-lee) *adverb*.

pragmatic (prag-MAT-ik) *adjective*, also given as **pragmatical**
treating things or making decisions from a practical point of view.

Related words: **pragmatism** (PRAG-mə-TIZ-əm), **pragmaticality** (prag-MAT-i-KAL-i-tee) and **pragmaticalness** (prag-MAT-i-kəl-nis) *all nouns*, **pragmatically** *adverb*.

prate (prayt) and **prattle** (PRAT-əl) *both verbs*
1. talk too much; chatter.
2. **prattle**, chatter in a childish way.

Related words: **prater** (PRAY-tər) *noun*, **pratingly** *adverb*; **prattler** (PRAT-lər) *noun*, **prattlingly** *adverb*.

prattle (PRAT-əl) *verb*

See **prate**.

precipitate (pri-SIP-i-tit) *adjective*
1. headlong, violently hurried.
2. of a person or action, hasty, rash; sudden.
3. *(verb)* (pri-SIP-i-TAYT) cause to happen suddenly or soon.

Do not confuse the adjective **precipitate** with **precipitous**, which see.

Related words: **precipitately** (pri-SIP-i-tit-lee) *adverb*, **precipitateness** (pri-SIP-i-tit-nis) and **precipitator** (pri-SIP-i-TAY-tər) *both nouns*, **precipitative** (pri-SIP-i-TAY-tiv) *adjective*.

precipitous (pri-SIP-i-təs) *adjective*
1. dangerously steep.
2. like a precipice.

The adjectives **precipitous** and **precipitate**—along with the corresponding adverbs **precipitously** and **precipitately**—are used interchangeably by writers and speakers who should know better. So prevalent is this confusion that permissive lexicographers, as one might expect, label the adjectives as synonyms in at least one sense. Well educated writers and their editors reject this practice, as should you. Reserve **precipitous** and **precipitously** for sentences in which the desired meaning is *dangerously steep* or *steeply*. Reserve **precipitate** and **precipitately** for sentences intended to convey the meaning of *sudden* and *suddenly*. Thus, you might write "They stopped just short of going over the rim of the **precipitous** cliff," and "They voted against making any **precipitate** decisions." Your editors will love you.

Related words: **precipitously** *adverb*, **precipitousness** *noun*.

preclude (pri-KLOOD) *verb*

1. exclude the possibility of.
2. prevent, forestall; debar.

Related words: **precludable** and **preclusive** (pri-KLOO-siv) *both adjectives*, **preclusion** (pri-KLOO-zhən) *noun*, **preclusively** *adverb*.

preponderate (pri-PON-də-RAYT) *verb*

surpass others in numbers, intensity, force, etc.

Related words: **preponderance** (pri-PON-dər-əns), **preponderation** (pri-PON-də-RAY-shən), and **preponderancy** (pri-PON-də-rən-see) *all nouns*; **preponderant** (pri-PON-dər-ənt) *adjective*, **preponderantly** *adverb*.

presage (PRES-ij) *noun*

1. an omen, a portent, a foreboding.
2. *(verb)* portend, foreshadow, also pronounced pri-SAYJ.

Related words: **presageful** *adjective*, **presagefully** *adverb*, **presager** *noun*.

prescience (PRESH-əns) *noun*

1. foreknowledge.
2. foresight.

Related words: **prescient** *adjective*, **presciently** *adverb*.

presentiment (pri-ZEN-tə-mənt) *noun*

a feeling that something is about to happen, especially something evil; a foreboding.

Related word: **presentimental** (pri-ZEN-tə-MEN-təl) *adjective*.

primer (PRIM-ər) *noun*
1. an elementary textbook.
2. (PRĪ-mər) a substance to prepare a surface for painting.
3. (PRĪ-mər) a detonator for explosives.

This entry is supplied primarily (no pun intended) to call attention to the correct pronunciations for the noun **primer** in its three meanings.

primeval (prī-MEE-vəl) *adjective*
1. of the earliest times of the world.
2. ancient.
3. primitive.

Related word: **primevally** *adverb*.

probative (PROH-bə-tiv) and **probatory** (PROH-bə-TOR-ee) *both adjectives*
1. providing proof.
2. designed to test or try something.

probatory (PROH-bə-TOR-ee) *adjective*

See **probative**.

probity (PROH-bi-tee) *noun*
1. honesty; integrity.
2. moral excellence.

proclivity (proh-KLIV-i-tee) *noun, plural* **proclivities**
1. a natural or habitual tendency.
2. an inclination.

profligate (PROF-li-git) *adjective*
1. recklessly wasteful or extravagant.
2. dissolute; immoral.

Related words: **profligacy** (PROF-li-gə-see) and **proligateness** (PROF-li-git-nis) *both nouns*, **profligately** *adverb*.

prolegomenon (PROH-lə-GOM-ə-NON) *noun, plural* **prolegomena** (PROH-lə-GOM-ə-nə)
1. preliminary matter in a book.
2. an introductory essay in a book.

Related word: **prolegomenous** (PROH-lə-GOM-ə-nəs) *adjective*.

prolix (proh-LIKS *or* PROH-liks) *adjective*
1. lengthy.
2. tediously wordy.

Related words: **prolixity** (proh-LIK-si-tee) and **prolixness** (proh-LIKS-nis) *both nouns*, **prolixly** (proh-LIKS-lee) *adverb*.

propinquity (proh-PING-kwi-tee) *noun*
nearness in place, kinship, disposition, or time.

propitiate (prə-PISH-ee-AYT) *verb*
1. win the favor or forgiveness of.
2. placate.

Related words: **propitiable** (prə-PISH-ee-ə-bəl), **propitiative** (prə-PISH-ee-AY-tiv), and **propitiatory** (prə-PISH-ee-ə-TOR-ee) *all adjectives*; **propitiation** (prə-PISH-ee-AY-shən) and **propitiator** (prə-PISH-ee-AY-tər) *both nouns*.

propitious (prə-PISH-əs) *adjective*
1. favorably inclined.
2. giving a good omen or a suitable opportunity.

Related words: **propitiously** *adverb*, **propitiousness** *noun*.

prostrate (PROS-trayt) *adjective*
1. lying face downward, especially as a sign of submission or humility.
2. lying in horizontal position.
3. helpless; overcome; physically exhausted.
4. *(verb)* cause to be prostrate; cast oneself face downward on the ground in humility or adoration.
5. *(verb)* reduce to physical exhaustion or helplessness.

The confusion of the adjective **prostrate**, *lying horizontal, helpless*, with the noun **prostate** (PROS-tayt), *a gland around the neck of the bladder in males*, is a boner we hear too often on radio talk shows. Remember to join in the laughter when you hear "He was **prostate** with grief." While **prostate** trouble may lead to grief, we all hope it does not leave the victim **prostrate**.

Related words: **prostration** (pros-TRAY-shən) and **prostrator** (PROS-tray-tər) *both nouns*, **prostrative** (PROS-trə-tiv) *adjective*.

protagonist (proh-TAG-ə-nist) *noun*
1. one of the chief contenders in a contest.

2. an advocate or champion of a cause etc.

3. the leading character in a literary work.

Related word: **protagonism** *noun.*

protean (PROH-tee-ən) *adjective*

1. taking many forms.

2. variable.

3. versatile.

Related word: **proteanism** (PROH-tee-ən-iz-əm) *noun.*

provenance (PROV-ə-nəns) *noun*
of a work of art etc., a place of origin.

proximate (PROK-sə-mit) *adjective*

1. nearest.

2. next before or after.

Related words: **proximately** *adverb,* **proximateness** and **proximation** (PROK-sə-MAY-shən) *both nouns.*

prurient (PRUUR-ee-ənt) *adjective*
having or arising from lewd thoughts.

Related words: **prurience** and **pruriency** *both nouns,* **pruriently** *adverb.*

puissant (PYOO-ə-sənt) *adjective*
having great power or strength; potent.

Related words: **puissance** *noun,* **puissantly** *adverb.*

punctilious (pungk-TIL-ee-əs) *adjective*
very careful to carry out duties or details of ceremony etc. correctly; conscientious.

Related words: **punctiliously** *adverb,* **punctiliousness** *noun.*

purulent (PYUUR-yə-lənt) *adjective*

1. containing or consisting of pus.

2. discharging pus.

Related words: **purulence** *noun,* **purulently** *adverb.*

pusillanimous (PYOO-sə-LAN-ə-məs) *adjective*

1. timid, faint-hearted.

2. cowardly.

Related words: **pusillanimity** (PYOO-sə-lə-NIM-i-tee) *noun*, **pusillanimously** (PYOO-sə-LAN-ə-məs-lee) *adverb*.

putative (PYOO-tə-tiv) *adjective*
reputed, supposed.

Related word: **putatively** *adverb*.

putrescent (pyoo-TRES-ənt) *adjective*
1. in process of decaying.
2. rotting.

Related words: **putrescence** and **putrescency** *both nouns*.

Pyrrhic (PIR-ik) **victory**
a victory gained at too great a cost.

Q

quash (kwosh) *verb*
1. annul; by legal authority, reject as not valid.
2. suppress or crush.

> Do not confuse **quash** with **squash**. Uprisings and indictments are **quashed**; hats and ripe grapes are **squashed**. But see **squelch**, which in one of its meanings is synonymous with **quash**.

querulous (KWER-ə-ləs) *adjective*
complaining, peevish

> Related words: **querulously** *adverb*, **querulousness** *noun*.

quidnunc (KWID-NUNGK) *noun*
1. a busybody.
2. a gossip.

quid pro quo (KWID proh KWOH), *plural* **quid pro quos** or **quids pro quo**
a thing given or taken in return for something.

quietus (kwī-EE-təs) *noun, plural* **quietuses**
1. final release from life, death.
2. a receipt given on payment of a debt.

quintessence (kwin-TES-əns) *noun*
1. an essence of a substance.
2. the essence or essential part of a theory, speech, condition, etc.
3. a perfect example of a quality.

Related words: **quintessential** (KWIN-tə-SEN-shəl) *adjective,* **quintessentially** (KWIN-tə-SEN-shee-əl-ee) *adverb.*

quisling (KWIZ-ling) *noun*
a traitor, especially one who collaborates with an enemy occupying his country.

quixotic (kwik-SOT-ik) *adjective,* also given as **quixotical** (kwik-SOT-i-kəl)
1. chivalrous and unselfish to an exaggerated degree.
2. impracticable, visionary.

Related word: **quixotically** *adverb.*

quondam (KWON-dəm) *adjective*
former; sometime; onetime.

quotidian (kwoh-TID-ee-ən) *adjective*
1. daily.
2. usual, everyday.
3. ordinary, commonplace; trivial.

Related words: **quotidianly** *adverb,* **quotidianness** *noun.*

R

rabid (RAB-id) *adjective*
1. fanatical.
2. raging, violently intense.
3. affected with rabies.

Related words: **rabidity** (rə-BID-i-tee) and **rabidness** (RAB-id-nis) *both nouns,* **rabidly** *adverb.*

raconteur (RAK-ən-TUR) *noun*
a person skilled in telling stories and anecdotes.

Related word: **raconteuse** (RAK-ən-TUZ) *noun,* a woman thus skilled.

raffish (RAF-ish) *adjective*
1. gaudily vulgar or cheap, tawdry.
2. engagingly nonconformist.
3. flashy, rakish.

Related words: **raffishly** *adverb,* **raffishness** *noun.*

raillery (RAY-lə-ree) *noun, plural* **railleries**
good-humored joking or teasing; banter.

rakish (RAY-kish) *adjective*
1. immoral or debauched.
2. debonair and jaunty in appearance or manner.

rale (rahl) *noun*
an abnormal sound perceived in the chest, indicating disease or congestion of the lungs.

rancor (RANG-kər) *noun*
1. bitter resentment, ill will.
2. hatred, malice.

Related words: **rancorous** (RANG-kər-əs) *adjective*, **rancorously** *adverb*, **rancorousness** *noun*.

randy (RAN-dee) *adjective*
lustful; eager for sexual gratification; lecherous.

Related word: **randiness** *noun*.

rankle (RANG-kəl) *verb*
cause lasting and bitter annoyance or resentment.

Related word: **ranklingly** *adverb*.

rapacious (rə-PAY-shəs) *adjective*
1. greedy and grasping, especially for money.
2. given to plundering and robbing others.

Related words: **rapaciously** *adverb*, **rapacity** (rə-PAS-i-tee) and **rapaciousness** (rə-PAY-shəs-nis) *both nouns*.

rapine (RAP-in) *noun*
1. plunder; pillage.
2. robbery.

rapprochement (RA-prohsh-MAHN) *noun*
the reestablishment of harmonious relations.

rara avis (RAIR-ə AY-vis)
a person or thing rarely encountered; a rarity.

ratiocination (RASH-ee-OS-ə-NAY-shən) *noun*
the use of logical processes and formal reasoning.

Related words: **ratiocinate** (RASH-ee-OS-ə-NAYT) *verb*, **ratiocinative** (RASH-ee-OS-i-NAY-tiv) *adjective*, **ratiocinator** (RASH-ee-OS-i-NAY-tər) *noun*.

rationale (RASH-ə-NAL) *noun*
1. a fundamental reason.
2. the logical basis of something.
3. a reasoned explanation of something.

raze (rayz) *verb*
1. destroy completely.
2. tear down to the ground.

Related word: **razer** *noun.*

rebarbative (ree-BAHR-bə-tiv) *adjective*
causing aversion or irritation; repellent.

recension (ri-SEN-shən) *noun*
1. an editorial revision of a literary work.
2. a work that has been editorially revised.

Related word: **recensionist** *noun.*

recherché (rə-shair-SHAY) *adjective*
1. devised or selected with great care.
2. very rare.
3. choice, precious; pretentious.

recidivist (ri-SID-ə-vist) *noun*
a person who continually commits crime and seems unable to be cured of criminal tendencies; a persistent offender.

Related words: **recidivism** (ri-SID-ə-VIZ-əm) *noun,* **recidivistic** (ri-SID-ə-VIS-tik) and **recidivous** (ri-SID-ə-vəs) *both adjectives.*

réclame (ray-KLAHM) *noun*
1. publicity.
2. notoriety.
3. public acclaim.

recondite (REK-ən-DĪT) *adjective*
1. of a subject, obscure.
2. of an author, writing about an obscure subject.

Related words: **reconditely** *adverb,* **reconditeness** *noun.*

recreant (REK-ree-ənt) *noun*
1. a coward.
2. a traitor.

Related words: **recreant** *adjective,* **recreantly** *adverb,* **recreance** and **recreancy** *both nouns.*

recriminate (ri-KRIM-ə-NAYT) *verb*
1. indulge in countercharges.
2. accuse in return.

Related words: **recrimination** (ri-KRIM-ə-NAY-shən) and **recriminator** (ri-KRIM-ə-NAY-tər) *both nouns*, **recriminative** (ri-KRIM-ə-NAY-tiv) and **recriminatory** (ri-KRIM-ə-nə-TOR-ee) *both adjectives.*

recrudesce (REE-kroo-DES) *verb*
of a disease or sore or hostile feeling, break out again.

Related words: **recrudescence** (REE-kroo-DES-əns) and **recrudescency** *both nouns*, **recrudescent** *adjective.*

recumbent (ri-KUM-bənt) *adjective*
1. lying down.
2. reclining.

Related words: **recumbence** and **recumbency** *both nouns*, **recumbently** *adverb.*

redact (ri-DAKT) *verb*
put into suitable literary form; edit.

Related words: **redaction** and **redactor** *both nouns*, **redactional** (ri-DAK-shən-əl) *adjective.*

redintegrate (red-IN-tə-GRAYT) *verb*
1. make whole again.
2. reestablish in a perfect state; renew.

Related words: **redintegration** (red-IN-tə-GRAY-shən) *noun*, **redintegrative** (red-IN-tə-GRAY-tiv) *adjective.*

redolent (RED-ə-lənt) *adjective*
1. having a strong smell, odorous.
2. having a pleasing smell, fragrant.
3. strongly suggestive, reminiscent.

Related works: **redolence** and **redolency** *both nouns*, **redolently** *adverb.*

redundant (ri-DUN-dənt) *adjective*
1. no longer needed; superfluous.
2. verbose, unnecessarily repetitive.

3. of equipment in a system, having more than the minimum needed for safe operation; back-up.

Related words: **redundancy** *noun*, **redundantly** *adverb*.

refectory (ri-FEK-tə-ree) *noun, plural* **refectories**
the dining hall of a monastery, college, or similar institution.

refractory (ri-FRAK-tə-ree) *adjective*
1. resisting control or discipline.
2. of a disease or other abnormal condition, not yielding to treatment.
3. of a substance, resistant to heat; hard to fuse or work.

Related words: **refractories** *plural noun* meaning *bricks used to line kilns*, **refractorily** *adverb*, **refractoriness** *noun*.

refulgent (ri-FUL-jənt) *adjective*
1. shining brightly, gleaming.
2. radiant.

Related words: **refulgence**, **refulgency**, and **refulgentness** *all nouns*; **refulgently** *adverb*.

regimen (REJ-ə-mən) *noun*
1. a prescribed course of exercise or way of life, especially a diet.
2. a government; a regime.

regretful (ri-GRET-fəl) *adjective*
full of regret, especially for something lost, done, gone, etc.

Do not confuse **regretful** with **regrettable**, which see.

Related words: **regretfully** *adverb*, **regretfulness** *noun*.

regrettable (ri-GRET-ə-bəl) *adjective*
1. causing or deserving regret.
2. unfortunate.

Do not confuse **regrettable** with **regretful**. Actions, accidents, errors, and the like may be **regrettable**. People may feel **regretful**. So while you will surely make **regrettable** mistakes from time to time and feel properly **regretful** about your lapses, choose correctly when you are considering whether to use **regretful** or **regrettable**.

Related words: **regrettableness** *noun*, **regrettably** *adverb*.

reify (REE-ə-Fī) *verb*
1. convert mentally into a thing.
2. materialize.

>Related word: **reification** (REE-ə-fi-KAY-shən) *noun*.

religiose (ri-LIJ-ee-OHS) *adjective*
unduly occupied with religion, excessively religious.

>Do not confuse **religiose** with **religious**, with a meaning easily understood. People who are **religious** are not necessarily **religiose**.

religious (ri-LIJ-əs) *adjective*

>See **religiose**.

reliquary (REL-i-KWER-ee) *noun, plural* **reliquaries**
a receptacle or a shrine for relics.

remanent (REM-ə-nənt) *adjective*
of a substance or electrical activity, remaining; residual.

>Related word: **remanence** *noun*.

remonstrate (ri-MON-strayt) *verb*
1. make a protest.
2. plead in protest.

>Related words: **remonstrance** (ri-MON-strəns), **remonstration** (REE-mon-STRAY-shən), and **remonstrator** (ri-MON-stray-tər) *all nouns*; **remonstrative** (ri-MON-strə-tiv) *adjective*; **remonstratively** (ri-MON-strə-tiv-lee) and **remonstratingly** (ri-MON-strayt-ing-lee) *both adverbs*.

renitent (REN-i-tənt) *adjective*
1. resistant to pressure.
2. persistently opposing; recalcitrant.

>Related words: **renitence** and **renitency**, *both nouns*.

repine (ri-PĪN) *verb*
1. be discontented.
2. fret.

>Related word: **repiner** *noun*.

retroussé (RE-troo-SAY) *adjective*
especially of the nose, turned up at the tip.

revenant (REV-ə-nənt) *noun*
one who returns from the dead or from exile etc.

revile (ri-VĪL) *verb*
criticize angrily in abusive language.
Related words: **revilement** and **reviler** *both nouns,* **revilingly**
adverb.

rhabdomantist (RAB-də-MAN-tist) *noun*
a person who practices divination by means of a rod or wand to
locate underground ore etc.; a dowser.
Related word: **rhabdomancy** (RAB-də-MAN-see) *noun.*

riparian (ri-PAIR-ee-ən) *adjective*
of or on a riverbank.

risible (RIZ-ə-bəl) *adjective*
1. of or relating to laughter.
2. causing laughter.
3. laughable, ludicrous, comical.
Related word: **risibility** (RIZ-ə-BIL-i-tee) *noun.*

rodomontade (ROD-ə-mon-TAYD) *noun*
1. boastful talk.
2. *(adjective)* boastful, bragging.
3. *(verb)* boast, brag.
4. *(verb)* rant.

roister (ROY-stər) *verb*
1. revel noisily.
2. act boisterously.
Related words: **roisterous** *adjective,* **roisterously** *adverb.*

rotund (roh-TUND) *adjective*
1. rounded, plump.
2. of the mouth, rounded in speaking or singing.
3. of speech etc., sonorous, full-toned.
Do not confuse **rotund** in sense 3 with **orotund**, which see.

While the two adjectives are similar in spelling and both are used to characterize sounds made by the human voice, they carry different meanings. **Orotund** is defined as *with full voice, imposing, dignified; pompous, pretentious.* **Rotund** in sense 3 means *sonorous, full-toned.* Close, but no cigar. Notice particularly the final words of the definition of **orotund**: *pompous, pretentious.* In this sense **orotund** is far from complimentary, while **rotund** in sense 3 indicates nothing but praise for the characteristic thus described. So take care when using these troublesome adjectives.

Related words: **rotundity** (roh-TUN-di-tee) and **rotundness** *both nouns*, **rotundly** *adverb*.

roustabout (ROWST-ə-BOWT) *noun*
an unskilled worker employed in an oil field, on the docks or, especially, in a circus.

rubicund (ROO-bə-KUND) *adjective*
of the complexion, red; ruddy.

Related word: **rubicundity** (ROO-bə-KUN-di-tee) *noun.*

rubric (ROO-brik) *noun*
1. a heading of a chapter, section, etc.
2. an explanatory note.
3. a direction indicating how something must be done.

Related words: **rubrician** (roo-BRISH-ən) and **rubrist** (ROO-brist) *both nouns.*

ruminant (ROO-mə-nənt) *noun*
1. an animal that chews the cud.
2. *(adjective)* chewing the cud, ruminative.
3. *(adjective)* contemplative, meditative.

Related word: **ruminantly** *adverb.*

ruminate (ROO-mə-NAYT) *verb*
1. chew the cud.
2. meditate, muse; ponder.

Related words: **rumination** (ROO-mə-NAY-shən) and **ruminator** (ROO-mə-NAY-tər) *both nouns*, **ruminative** (ROO-mə-NAY-tiv) *adjective*, **ruminatively** (ROO-mə-NAY-tiv-lee) *adverb.*

rusticate (RUS-ti-KAYT) *verb*
1. settle or vacation in the country.
2. live a rural life.

Related words: **rustication** (RUS-ti-KAY-shən) and **rusticator** (RUS-ti-KAY-tər) *both nouns.*

S

sacerdotal (SAS-ər-DOHT-əl) *adjective*
1. of priests or the priesthood.
2. priestly.

Related words: **sacerdotalism** (SAS-ər-DOHT-əl-IZ-əm) and **sacerdotalist** (SAS-ər-DOHT-əl-ist) *both nouns,* **sacerdotally** *adverb.*

sagacious (sə-GAY-shəs) *adjective*
showing wisdom in one's understanding and judgment of things; wise.

Related words: **sagacity** (sə-GAS-i-tee) and **sagaciousness** (sə-GAY-shəs-nis) *both nouns,* **sagaciously** *adverb.*

salacious (sə-LAY-shəs) *adjective*
1. erotic.
2. lewd, grossly indecent, obscene.

Related words: **salaciously** *adverb,* **salaciousness** *noun.*

salubrious (sə-LOO-bree-əs) *adjective*
health-promoting; health-giving; healthful.

Related words: **salubriously** *adverb,* **salubriousness** and **salubrity** (sə-LOO-bri-tee) *both nouns.*

salutary (SAL-yə-TER-ee) *adjective*
producing a beneficial or wholesome effect.

Related words: **salutarily** (SAL-yə-TER-ə-lee) *adverb,* **salutariness** (SAL-yə-TER-ee-nis) *noun.*

sanctimonious (SANGK-tə-MOH-nee-əs) *adjective*
making a hypocritical show of righteousness or piety.

Related words: **sanctimoniously** *adverb*, **sanctimoniousness** and **sanctimony** (SANGK-tə-MOH-nee) *both nouns*.

sang-froid (sahn-FRWAH) *noun*
1. calmness in the face of danger or difficulty.
2. composure; self-possession.

sanguinary (SANG-gwə-NER-ee) *adjective*
1. full of bloodshed.
2. bloodthirsty; savage.

Do not confuse **sanguinary** with **sanguine**, which see.

Related words: **sanguinarily** (SANG-gwə-NER-i-lee) *adverb*, **sanguinariness** *noun*.

sanguine (SANG-gwin) *adjective*
1. hopeful, optimistic.
2. confident.

Do not confuse **sanguine**, *optimistic, hopeful,* with **sanguinary**, *bloodthirsty.* The resemblance of the two words sets a trap for the unwary. Remember that it never hurts to be **sanguine**, but **sanguinary** is a horse of a different color — red, for blood.

Related words: **sanguinely** *adverb*, **sanguinness** and **sanguinity** (sang-GWIN-i-tee) *both nouns*.

sapid (SAP-id) *adjective*
1. having flavor, especially agreeable flavor.
2. palatable, savory.
3. of speech or writing, agreeable; interesting.

Related words: **sapidity** (sə-PID-i-tee), **sapidness** (SAP-id-nis) *both nouns*.

sapient (SAY-pee-ənt) *adjective*, also given as **sapiential** (SAY-pee-EN-shəl)
having or pretending to have great wisdom.

Related words: **sapience** and **sapiency** *both nouns*, **sapiently** *adverb*.

sarcophagus (sahr-KOF-ə-gəs) *noun, plural* **sarcophagi** (sahr-KOF-ə-JĪ) *or* **sarcophaguses**

a stone coffin, especially one bearing sculpture, inscriptions, etc.

Do not confuse the noun **sarcophagus** with the adjective **sarcophagous** (sahr-KOF-ə-gəs), which means *carnivorous, flesh-eating*.

sardonic (sahr-DON-ik) *adjective*

1. humorous in a grim or sarcastic way.
2. cynical.

Related words: **sardonically** *adverb*, **sardonicism** (sahr-DON-i-siz-əm) *noun*.

satiate (SAY-shee-AYT) *verb*

1. satisfy an appetite fully.
2. glut or cloy with an excess of something.

Related words: **satiation** (SAY-shee-AY-shən) and **satiety** (sə-TĪ-i-tee) *both nouns*.

saturnine (SAT-ər-NĪN) *adjective*

of a person or his looks, having a gloomy and forbidding appearance.

Related words: **saturninely** *adverb*, **saturninity** (SAT-ər-NIN-i-tee) and **saturnineness** (SAT-ər-NĪN-nis) *both nouns*.

scabrous (SKAB-rəs) *adjective*

1. indecent, salacious.
2. behaving indecently or immorally.
3. having a rough surface.
4. of a subject or situation, hard to handle with decency; requiring tactful treatment.

Related words: **scabrously** *adverb*, **scabrousness** *noun*.

scapegoat (SKAYP-GOHT) *noun*

a person who is made to bear blame or punishment that should rightly fall on others.

Do not confuse **scapegoat** with **scapegrace**, which see.

Related words: **scapegoat** *verb*, **scapegoating** and **scapegoatism** (SKAYP-goh-TIZ-əm) *both nouns*.

scapegrace (SKAYP-GRAYS) *noun*
1. a rascal.
2. a person who is constantly getting into trouble.

Do not confuse **scapegrace** with **scapegoat**. The former is a relatively uncommon word, the latter an all too common word. A **scapegrace** is a *rascal, constantly in trouble,* and deserving of blame; a **scapegoat** is the *undeserving recipient of blame.* Thus, it would appear that anyone who must be called one thing or another may prefer to become a **scapegoat** rather than a **scapegrace**, since **scapegoats** are the victims of people of evil intent, and **scapegraces** earn their pejorative characterizations by virtue of their undesirable proclivities. So you must take care when using either of these words to choose the one that is correct for the meaning you intend to convey. And understand that **scapegraces** are often unjustifiably made **scapegoats** when wagging tongues are seeking to fix blame on someone.

scarify (SKAR-ə-FĪ) *verb*
1. make slight surgical cuts in skin or tissue.
2. of a person, pain by merciless criticism.
3. of garden soil etc., loosen the surface.

Related words: **scarifier** and **scarification** (SKAR-ə-fi-KAY-shən) *both nouns.*

schadenfreude (SHAHD-ən-FROY-də) *noun*
malicious satisfaction felt at the misfortunes of someone else.

sciamachy (sī-AM-ə-kee) *noun, plural* **sciamachies**
an act of fighting with shadows or an imaginary enemy.

sciolist (SĪ-ə-list) *noun*
a superficial pretender to knowledge.

Related words: **sciolism** (SĪ-ə-LIZ-əm) *noun,* **sciolistic** (SĪ-ə-LIS-tik) *adjective.*

scoliosis (SKOH-lee-OH-sis) *noun*
an abnormal lateral curvature of the spine.

Related word: **scoliotic** (SKOH-lee-OT-ik) *adjective.*

scourge (skurj) *noun*
1. a person or thing regarded as a great affliction.

2. a whip for flogging people.

3. *(verb)* flog with a whip.

4. *(verb)* afflict greatly.

Related words: **scourger** *noun,* **scourgingly** *adverb.*

scurrilous (SKUR-ə-ləs) *adjective*

1. abusive and insulting.

2. coarsely humorous or derisive.

Related words: **scurrility** (skə-RIL-i-tee) and **scurrilousness** (SKUR-ə-ləs-nis) *both nouns,* **scurrilously** *adverb.*

sedulous (SEJ-ə-ləs) *adjective*
diligent and persevering; assiduous.

Related words: **sedulously** *adverb,* **sedulousness** *noun.*

self-abnegation (SELF-AB-ni-GAY-shən) *noun*

See **abnegate**.

semiology (SEE-mee-OL-ə-jee) *noun*
the branch of linguistics concerned with signs and symbols.

Related words: **semiologic** (SEE-mee-ə-LOJ-ik) and **semiological** *both adjectives,* **semiologist** (SEE-mee-OL-ə-jist) *noun.*

sempiternal (SEM-pi-TUR-nəl) *adjective*
everlasting; eternal.

Related word: **sempiternally** *adverb.*

senescent (si-NES-ənt) *adjective*
growing old; aging.

Related word: **senescence** *noun.*

sensual (SEN-shoo-əl) *adjective*

1. physical.

2. gratifying to the body.

3. indulging oneself with physical pleasures.

4. worldly, materialistic, irreligious.

Do not confuse **sensual** with **sensuous**, which see.

Related words: **sensually** *adverb,* **sensualism** (SEN-shoo-ə-LIZ-əm), **sensualist,** and **sensuality** (SEN-shoo-AL-i-tee) *all nouns.*

sensuous (SEN-shoo-əs) *adjective*
affecting or appealing to the senses, especially by beauty or delicacy.

Do not confuse **sensuous** with **sensual**. While both adjectives refer to experience gained through the senses, they differ markedly in interpretation. **Sensual** often carries an unfavorable connotation, for example, in such phrases as *sensual excesses* and *sensual sunbathing in which one's curves are displayed*. By way of contrast, **sensuous** offers such phrases as *sensuous music* and *sensuous poetry*, and no one ever came to a sordid end by indulging in the enjoyment of music or poetry that appeals to the senses.

Related words: **sensuously** *adverb*, **sensuosity** (SEN-shoo-OS-i-tee) and **sensuousness** *both nouns*.

sententious (sen-TEN-shəs) *adjective*
1. putting on an air of wisdom.
2. dull and moralizing.

Related words: **sententiously** *adverb*, **sententiousness** and **sententiosity** (sen-TEN-shee-OS-i-tee) *both nouns*.

sepulcher (SEP-əl-kər) *noun*
a tomb.

Related words: **sepulchral** (sə-PUL-krəl) *adjective*, **sepulchrally** (sə-PUL-krə-lee) *adverb*.

sepulture (SEP-əl-chər) *noun*
burial, interment.

Related word: **sepultural** (sə-PUL-chər-əl) *adjective*.

serendipity (SER-ən-DIP-i-tee) *noun*
1. the making of pleasant discoveries by accident.
2. the knack of doing this.

Related words: **serendipiter**, **serendipitist**, and **serendipper** *all nouns*; **serendipitous** *adjective*.

sesquipedalian (SES-kwi-pi-DAYL-yən) *adjective*
1. of a word, having many syllables.
2. of a writer, tending to use long words.

Related words: **sesquipedalianism** (SES-kwi-pi-DAYL-yən-iz-əm) and **sesquipedality** (SES-kwi-pi-DAL-i-tee) *both nouns.*

shibboleth (SHIB-ə-lith) *noun*

1. an old slogan or principle that is still considered essential by some members of a party or group.
2. a test word, principle, behavior, or opinion whose use reveals one's party, nationality, orthodoxy, etc.

sibyl (SIB-əl) *noun*

1. a fortune-teller; a prophetess.
2. a witch.
3. one of the women of classical legend who were supposed to prophesy under the influence of a god.

Related word: **sibylline** (SIB-ə-LĪN) *adjective.*

simplistic (sim-PLIS-tik) *adjective*
tending to simplify something unjustifiably.

Anyone who listens to talk radio or reads letters written to newspaper editors knows there is an army of poor speakers and writers for whom the elegant adjective **simplistic** holds a fatal fascination—fatal because these speakers and writers mistakenly use **simplistic** as a synonym for **simple**. And one thing **simplistic** is not is a synonym for **simple**. Anyone who uses **simplistic** must be certain he or she intends to convey the meaning of *tending to simplify something unjustifiably.* The adverb *unjustifiably* is the red flag alerting us to the negative connotation of **simplistic**. For example, telling Americans that by eliminating the Internal Revenue Service we will solve all our economic problems is usually taken by rational people to be an example of a **simplistic** proposal. And there are, of course, many other examples of **simplistic** reasoning. So remember that when you describe some idea or proposal as **simplistic**, you are criticizing it as you characterize it.

Related words: **simplistically** *adverb*, **simplism** (SIM-pliz-əm) *noun.*

Sisyphean (SIS-ə-FEE-ən) *adjective*

1. everlastingly laborious and unavailing.
2. of or pertaining to Sisyphus who, in Greek legend, was con-

demned to roll a huge boulder to the top of a hill in Hades, but every time he reached the summit, the boulder slipped out of his grasp and rolled down again.

sluggard (SLUG-ərd) *noun*
a slow or lazy person.

Related words: **sluggard** and **sluggardly** *both adjectives*, **sluggardliness** *noun*.

smegma (SMEG-mə) *noun*
a thick, cheeselike secretion in the folds of the skin, especially in the foreskin.

Related word: **smegmatic** (smeg-MA-tik) *adjective*.

sobriquet (SOH-brə-KAY) *noun*
a nickname.

Related word: **sobriquetical** (SOH-brə-KET-i-kəl) *adjective*

sodomy (SOD-ə-mee) *noun*
a copulation-like act between male persons or with a member of the opposite sex or between a person and an animal.

Related words: **sodomite** (SOD-ə-MĪT) **sodomist** (SOD-ə-mist) *both nouns*, **sodomitical** (SOD-ə-MIT-i-kəl) *adjective*, **sodomitically** *adverb*.

soi-disant (swah-dee-ZAHN) *adjective*, French
1. self-styled.
2. so-called.
3. pretended.

soigné (swahn-YAY) *adjective, feminine* **soignée**
1. well-groomed and sophisticated.
2. carefully designed and prepared.

solecism (SOL-ə-SIZ-əm) *noun*
1. a mistake in the use of language.
2. an offense against good manners or etiquette.

Do not confuse **solecism** with **solipsism**, which see.

Related words: **solecist** (SOL-ə-sist) *noun*, **solecistic** (SOL-ə-SIS-tik) and **solecistical** *both adjectives*, **solecistically** *adverb*.

solicitous (sə-LIS-i-təs) *adjective*
anxious and concerned about a person's welfare or comfort.

Related words: **solicitously** *adverb*, **solicitousness** and **solicitude** (sə-LIS-i-TOOD) *both nouns.*

solipsism (SOL-ip-SIZ-əm) *noun*
1. the philosophical theory that the self is the only knowable, or the only existent, thing.
2. egoistic self-absorption.

The nouns **solecism** and **solipsism** are relatively uncommon words, sharing nothing but similarity of spelling and pronunciation, yet careless writers and speakers confuse the words. One meaning of **solecism** is *a mistake in the use of language,* and one meaning of **solipsism** is *egoistic self-absorption.* If you intend to use either of these words, keep their meanings firmly in mind so you will not be misled by superficial similarities. And while you avoid **solecisms** in your writing, beware of falling prey to **solipsism.**

Related words: **solipsist** (SOL-ip-sist) and **solipsistic** (SOL-ip-SIS-tik) *both adjectives,* **solipsist** *noun.*

somnambulism (som-NAM-byə-LIZ-əm) *noun*
sleepwalking.

Related words: **somnambulant** (som-NAM-byə-lənt) and **somnambulistic** (som-NAM-byə-LIS-tik) *both adjectives,* **somnambulate** (som-NAM-byə-LAYT) *verb,* **somnambulation** (som-NAM-byə-LAY-shən) and **somnambulist** (som-NAM-byə-list) *both nouns.*

somnolent (SOM-nə-lənt) *adjective*
sleepy, drowsy; asleep.

Related words: **somnolence** and **somnolency** *both nouns,* **somnolently** *adverb.*

sonorous (sə-NOR-əs) *adjective*
1. giving a deep powerful sound; resonant.
2. of language or diction, high-flown, grandiloquent.

Related words: **sonority** and **sonorousness** *nouns,* **sonorously** *adverb.*

sophism (SOF-iz-əm) *noun*
a false argument, especially one intended to deceive.

Related words: **sophist** (SOF-ist) *noun*, **sophistic** (sə-FIS-tik) and **sophistical** *both adjectives*, **sophistically** *adverb*.

sophistry (SOF-ə-stree) *noun, plural* **sophistries**
clever and subtle but perhaps misleading reasoning.

soporific (SOP-ə-RIF-ik) *adjective*
1. tending to produce sleep.
2. *(noun)* a medicinal substance that produces sleep.

Related word: **soporifically** *adverb*.

sororicide (sə-ROR-ə-SĪD) *noun*
1. the act of killing one's sister.
2. a person who commits sororicide.

Related word: **sororicidal** (sə-ROR-ə-SĪD-əl) *adjective*.

soubrette (soo-BRET) *noun*
1. an actress or opera singer playing a maidservant or similar character, especially with the implication of pertness or coquetry.
2. the role itself.
3. any lively or pert young woman.

Related word: **soubrettish** *adjective*.

soupçon (soop-SAWN) *noun*
a very small quantity; a trace; a dash.

specious (SPEE-shəs) *adjective*
seeming good or sound at first sight but lacking real merit.

Related words: **speciously** *adverb*, **speciousness** *noun*.

splenetic (spli-NET-ik) *adjective*
1. of a person, ill-tempered; peevish, irascible.
2. of the spleen.

Related word: **splenetically** *adverb*.

spoonerism (SPOO-nə-RIZ-əm) *noun*
the interchange of the initial letters of two words, usually as a slip of the tongue.

squash (skwosh) *verb*
This verb is well understood and is supplied merely to call attention to the difference between **squash** and **quash**, which see.

squelch (skwelch) *verb*
1. silence, as with a crushing reply.
2. suppress, quell; quash.

Notice that **squelch** in its second sense is synonymous with **quash**, which see.

Related words: **squelcher** *noun*, **squelchingly** *adverb*, **squelchingness** *noun*.

stanch (stawnch) *verb*
1. restrain the flow of (blood etc.).
2. restrain the flow of blood from (a wound etc.).

Do not confuse **stanch** with **staunch**, which see.

Related words: **stanchable** *adjective*, **stancher** *noun*.

stationary (STAY-shə-NER-ee) *adjective*
1. not moving, not movable.
2. unchanging in condition or quantity etc.

Do not confuse the adjective **stationary** with the noun **stationery**. Both are pronounced identically, but there the similarity ends. **Stationery** is defined as *writing materials, such as paper, envelopes, and the like.*

staunch (stawnch) *adjective*
firm in attitude, opinion, or loyalty.

The adjective **staunch** and the verb **stanch** are frequently confused. As you can see, the two words are pronounced identically, but listeners alert to the context in which they hear the words have no trouble. It is when encountering the words in a piece of writing that trouble may arise for readers. Beginning far back in the history of the language, the two words were merely spelling variants, used interchangeably, so writers had nothing to worry about. In the 20th century, however, **staunch** and **stanch** began to be treated as different words, the first meaning *firm in attitude etc.*, the second meaning *restrain a flow*. Thus, even though some permissive dictionaries still may treat the two words as spelling variants, one of the things you must do as a careful writer is use **staunch** and **stanch** correctly. Remember to be **staunch** in your most cherished beliefs, and to **stanch** the flow of blood whenever you cut yourself badly. Also remember that **staunch** is an adjective, and **stanch** is a verb.

Related words: **staunchly** *adverb*, **staunchness** *noun*.

steatopygia (stee-AT-ə-PĪ-jee-ə) *noun*
excessive development of fat on the buttocks, especially of women.

Related words: **steatopygic** (stee-AT-ə-PIJ-ik) and **steatopygous** (stee-AT-ə-PĪ-gəs) *both adjectives*.

stratagem (STRAT-ə-jəm) *noun*
1. a cunning method of achieving something.
2. a piece of trickery.

Related words: **stratagemical** (STRAT-ə-JEM-i-kəl) *adjective*, **stratagemically** *adverb*.

stratum (STRAT-əm) *noun, plural* **strata** (STRAT-ə) and **stratums**
1. a social level or class.
2. one of a series of layers, especially of rock in Earth's crust.

Many students of English style have remarked on the increasing use of **strata** as a singular, but editors and careful writers use it only as a plural. Until poor usage overwhelms the conventional use of **strata** as a plural, you would do well to use **stratum** consistently as a singular, and **strata** or **stratums** as plurals.

Related word: **stratous** *adjective*.

stricture (STRIK-chər) *noun*
1. a remark or comment expressing criticism or condemnation.
2. an abnormal constriction of a tubelike part of the body.

Related words: **striction** (STRIK-shən) *noun*, **strictured** (STRIK-chərd) *adjective*.

stridulate (STRIJ-ə-LAYT) *verb*
of a cricket or cicada etc., make a shrill and grating sound by rubbing parts of the body together.

Related words: **stridulation** (STRIJ-ə-LAY-shən) *noun*, **stridulatory** (STRIJ-ə-lə-TOR-ee) and **stridulous** (STRIJ-ə-ləs) *both adjectives*.

stultify (STUL-tə-FĪ) *verb*
impair or make ineffective.

Related words: **stultification** (STUL-ti-fi-KAY-shən) and **stultifier** (STUL-ti-FĪ-ər) *both nouns,* **stultifyingly** (STUL-ti-FĪ-ing-lee) *adverb.*

sublimate (SUB-lə-MAYT) *verb*
divert the energy of (a primitive impulse) into a culturally higher activity.

Related words: **sublimable** (SUB-lə-mə-bəl) and **sublimational** (SUB-lə-MAY-shə-nəl) *both adjectives,* **sublimableness** (SUB-lə-mə-bəl-nis) and **sublimation** (SUB-lə-MAY-shən) *both nouns.*

subliminal (sub-LIM-ə-nəl) *adjective*
below the threshold of consciousness.

Related word: **subliminally** *adverb.*

succubus (SUK-yə-bəs) *noun, plural* **succubi** (SUK-yə-bī); also given as **succuba** (SUK-yə-bə), *plural* **succubae** (SUK-yə-bee)
1. a female demon said to have sexual intercourse with sleeping men.
2. any evil spirit.

sudorific (SOO-də-RIF-ik) *adjective*
1. causing sweating.
2. *(noun)* a drug that induces sweating.

suggestible (səg-JES-tə-bəl) *adjective*
1. easily influenced by people's suggestions.
2. that may be suggested.

Do not confuse **suggestible** with **suggestive**, which see.

Related words: **suggestibility** (səg-JES-tə-BIL-i-tee) and **suggestibleness** (səg-JES-tə-bəl-nis) *both nouns,* **suggestibly** (səg-JES-tə-blee) *adverb.*

suggestive (səg-JES-tiv) *adjective*
1. tending to convey an indecent or improper meaning; risqué.
2. conveying a suggestion.

Do not confuse **suggestive** with **suggestible**. The confusion that can result from careless use of these two adjectives gives us a wonderful example of the difference a suffix can make. The adjective **suggestive** is most often used in the sense of *tending to convey an indecent or improper meaning,* while **suggestible** is most often used in the sense of *easily influenced by people's suggestions.* Facial expressions and activities may be **suggestive**, while people, their ideas, their thoughts, and the like may be **suggestible**. Be careful in your use of these adjectives.

Related words: **suggestively** *adverb*, **suggestiveness** *noun*.

sui generis (SOO-ee JEN-ə-ris), Latin
1. of its, his, her, their own kind.
2. one of a kind; unique.

superannuate (SOO-pər-AN-yoo-AYT) *verb*
1. retire (an employee) with a pension because of age or infirmity.
2. discard (something) as too old for further use.

Related words: **superannuated** *adjective*, **superannuation** (SOO-pər-AN-yoo-AY-shən) *noun*.

supercilious (SOO-pər-SIL-ee-əs) *adjective*
1. with an air of superiority.
2. haughty and scornful.

Related words: **superciliously** *adverb*, **superciliousness** *noun*.

supererogation (SOO-pər-ER-ə-GAY-shən) *noun*
the doing of more than is required by duty.

Related words: **supererogate** (SOO-pər-ER-ə-GAYT) *verb*, **supererogatory** (SOO-pər-ə-ROG-ə-TOR-ee) *adjective*, **supererogatorily** *adverb*, **supererogator** (SOO-pər-ER-ə-GAY-tər) *noun*.

supernal (suu-PUR-nəl) *adjective*
1. heavenly, divine.
2. lofty.

Related word: **supernally** *adverb*.

supervene (SOO-pər-VEEN) *verb*
occur as an interruption or change from some condition or process.

Related words: **supervenience** (SOO-pər-VEEN-yəns) and **supervention** (SOO-pər-VEN-shən) *both nouns*, **supervenient** (SOO-pər-VEEN-yənt) *adjective*.

supine (soo-PĪN) *adjective*
1. lying face upward.
2. not inclined to take action.
3. indolent.

Related words: **supinely** *adverb*, **supineness** *noun*.

suppliant (SUP-lee-ənt) *noun*
a person asking humbly for something; a supplicant.

Related words: **suppliant** *adjective*, **suppliantly** *adverb*, **suppliantness** *noun*.

suppurate (SUP-yə-RAYT) *verb*
form pus; fester.

Related words: **suppuration** (SUP-yə-RAY-shən) *noun*, **suppurative** (SUP-yə-RAY-tiv) *adjective*.

surcease (sur-SEES) *noun*
end, cessation.

susurration (SOO-sə-RAY-shən) *noun*
1. whispering; murmuring.
2. rustling.

Related words: **susurrant** (suu-SUR-ənt) and **susurrous** (suu-SUR-əs) *both adjectives*, **susurrus** (suu-SUR-əs) *noun*.

svelte (svelt) *adjective*
1. of a person or figure, slender and graceful; lissome, lithe.
2. suave, urbane.

sybarite (SIB-ə-RĪT) *noun*
a person who is excessively fond of comfort and luxury.

Related words: **sybaritic** (SIB-ə-RIT-ik) and **sybaritical** *both adjectives*, **sybaritically** *adverb*, **sybaritism** (SIB-ə-ri-TIZ-əm) *noun*.

sycophant (SIK-ə-fənt) *noun*
1. a person who tries to win people's favor by flattering them.
2. a parasite.

Related words: **sycophancy** (SIK-ə-fən-see) and **sycophantism** *both nouns*; **sycophantic** (SIK-ə-FAN-tik), **sycophantical**, and **sycophantish** *all adjectives*; **sycophantically** (SIK-ə-FAN-tik-ə-lee) and **sycophantishly** (SIK-ə-FAN-tish-lee) *both adverbs*.

symbiosis (SIM-bee-OH-sis) *noun, plural* **symbioses** (SIM-bee-OH-seez)
the association of two different organisms living attached to each
other or one within the other to their mutual advantage.

Related words: **symbiotic** (SIM-bee-OT-ik) and **symbiotical** *both
adjectives*, **symbiotically** *adverb*.

sympathy (SIM-pə-thee) *noun*

See **empathy**.

synecdoche (si-NEK-də-kee) *noun*
a figure of speech in which a part is used for the whole, or vice
versa; or the less comprehensive is used for the more comprehensive, or vice versa.

Related words: **synecdochic** (SIN-ik-DOK-ik) and **synecdochical**
(SIN-ik-DOK-i-kəl) *both adjectives*, **synecdochically** (SIN-ik-
DOK-ik-ə-lee) *adverb*.

synergism (SIN-ər-JIZ-əm) *noun*, also given as **synergy** (SIN-ər-jee),
plural **synergies** (SIN-ər-jeez)
the combined effect of drugs, contributions, efforts, etc. that
exceeds the sum of their individual effects.

Related words: **synergist** (SIN-ər-jist) *noun*; **synergetic** (SIN-ər-
JET-ik), **synergistic** (SIN-ər-JIS-tik), and **synergic** (si-NUR-jik) *all
adjectives*; **synergistically** (SIN-ər-JIS-ti-kə-lee) *adverb*.

T

tabula rasa (TAB-yə-lə RAH-sə)
1. a blank tablet, especially the human mind at birth viewed as having no innate ideas.
2. anything existing undisturbed in its original state.
3. anything restored to its original state; a clean slate.

taciturn (TAS-i-TURN) *adjective*
1. habitually saying very little, uncommunicative.
2. reserved in speech.

Related words: **taciturnity** (TAS-i-TUR-ni-tee) *noun*, **taciturnly** (TAS-i-TURN-lee) *adverb*.

talisman (TAL-is-mən) *noun, plural* **talismans**
an object supposed to work wonders or to bring its possessor good luck.

Related words: **talismanic** (TAL-is-MAN-ik) and **talismanical** *both adjectives*, **talismanically** *adverb*.

tarantism (TA-rən-TIZ-əm) *noun*
a mania characterized by an irresistible urge to dance, popularly and incorrectly supposed to result from the bite of a tarantula.

Related word: **tarantist** (TA-rən-tist) *noun*.

tartuffe (tahr-TUUF) *noun*
a religious hypocrite, from the name of the central character in *Tartuffe*, a 17th-century comedy by the French playwright Molière.

Related word: **tartuffery** (tahr-TUUF-ə-ree) *noun*, **tartuffian** (tahr-TUUF-ee-ən) *adjective*.

tauromachy (taw-ROM-ə-kee) *noun*
the art of bullfighting.

Related word: **tauromachian** (TOR-ə-MAY-kee-ən) *adjective*.

tautology (taw-TOL-ə-jee) *noun*, *plural* **tautologies**
saying of the same thing twice over in different words, especially as a fault of style.

Related words: **tautological** (TAW-tə-LOJ-i-kəl), **tautologic**, and **tautologous** (taw-TOL-ə-gəs) *all adjectives*; **tautologically** and **tautologously** *both adverbs*; **tautologist** (taw-TOL-ə-jist) *noun*.

taxonomy (tak-SON-ə-mee) *noun*
the principles or science of classification, especially in biology.

Related words: **taxonomic** (TAK-sə-NOM-ik) and **taxonomical** *both adjectives*, **taxonomically** *adverb*, **taxonomist** (tak-SON-ə-mist) and **taxonomer** *both nouns*.

temerarious (TEM-ə-RAIR-ee-əs) *adjective*
reckless; rash.

Related words: **temerariously** *adjective*, **temerariousness** and **temerity** (tə-MER-i-tee) *both nouns*.

tendentious (ten-DEN-shəs) *adjective*, also given as **tendential** (ten-DEN-shəl)
1. of a speech or piece of writing etc., aimed at helping a cause.
2. exhibiting partiality.

Related words: **tendentially** *adverb*, **tendentiousness** *noun*.

tenebrific (TEN-ə-BRIF-ik) *adjective*
1. producing darkness.
2. obscuring.

tenuous (TEN-yoo-əs) *adjective*
1. having little substance or validity.
2. of slight significance.
3. very thin in form or consistency.

Related words: **tenuously** *adverb*, **tenuousness** and **tenuity** (tə-NOO-i-tee) *both nouns*.

tergiversate (TUR-ji-vər-SAYT) *verb*
1. turn one's back on one's party, cause, etc.
2. make evasive or conflicting statements; equivocate.

Related words: **tergiversation** (TUR-ji-vər-SAY-shən) **tergiversator** (TUR-ji-vər-SAY-tər), and **tergiversant** (TUR-ji-VUR-sənt) *all nouns*; **tergiversatory** (TUR-ji-VUR-sə-TOR-ee) *adjective*.

termagant (TUR-mə-gənt) *noun*
a shrewish bullying woman, a virago.

Related word: **termagant** *adjective*, meaning *shrewish*; *bullying*; **termagantly** *adverb*.

tessera (TES-ər-ə) *noun, plural* **tesserae** (TES-ə-ree)
a small cubical block of marble, glass, etc. used in mosaic.

thaumaturge (THAW-mə-TURJ) *noun*
1. a worker of miracles.
2. a wonder-worker.
3. a magician.

Related words: **thaumaturgic** (THAW-mə-TUR-jik) and **thaumaturgical** *both adjectives*, **thaumaturgy** (THAW-mə-TUR-jee) *noun*.

thrall (thrawl) *noun*
1. bondage, servitude.
2. captivity.
3. a slave of or to a person or thing.

Related word: **thralldom** (THRAWL-dəm) *noun*.

threnody (THREN-ə-dee) *noun, plural* **threnodies**
1. a song of lamentation, especially on a person's death; a dirge.
2. an elegy.

Related words: **threnodial** (thri-NOH-dee-əl) and **threnodic** (thri-NOD-ik) *both adjectives*, **threnodist** (THREN-ə-dist).

tinnitus (ti-NĪ-təs) *noun*
an abnormal condition of ringing or similar sensation in the ears.

titillate (TIT-əl-AYT) *verb*
1. excite or stimulate pleasantly.
2. tickle.

Do not confuse **titillate** with **titivate**, which see.

Related words: **titillatingly** (TIT-əl-AYT-ing-lee) *adverb*, **titillation** (TIT-əl-AY-shən) *noun*, **titillative** (TIT-əl-AY-tiv) *adjective*.

titivate (TIT-ə-VAYT) *verb*, also given as **tittivate**

1. spruce up.
2. adorn.
3. put the finishing touches to.

The temptation to treat **titivate** and **titillate** as synonyms is apparently so strong that some dictionaries list **titivate** as a synonym for the much older word **titillate**, when the only connection between the two verbs is their similarity of spelling. **Titillate** means *tickle*, and **titivate** means *spruce up*. In your own writing and speech, you should retain the distinction between the words, always keeping in mind that mistaken use of **titivate** will **titillate** educated readers and listeners.

Related words: **titivation** (TIT-ə-VAY-shən) and **titivator** (TIT-ə-VAY-tər) *both nouns*.

titubation (TICH-uu-BAY-shən) *noun*

1. unsteadiness, especially as caused by a nervous disease.
2. staggering.

Related word: **titubant** (TICH-uu-bənt) *adjective*.

tocsin (TOK-sin) *noun*

1. a signal of disaster.
2. a bell rung as an alarm.

tonsure (TON-shər) *noun*

1. the shaving of the top or all of the head of a person entering certain priesthoods or monastic orders.
2. the part of the head left bare after being shaved in this way.

Related word: **tonsure** *verb*, meaning *subject to tonsure*.

toothsome (TOOTH-səm) *adjective*

1. pleasant to eat; palatable.
2. attractive.
3. voluptuous.

Related words: **toothsomely** *adverb*, **toothsomeness** *noun*.

torpid (TOR-pid) *adjective*
sluggish and inactive; lethargic.

Related words: **torpidity** (tor-PID-i-tee), **torpidness** (TOR-pid-nis), and **torpor** (TOR-pər) *all nouns;* **torpidly** *adverb.*

tortuous (TOR-choo-əs) *adjective*
1. full of twists and turns.
2. of policy etc., not straightforward; devious; circuitous.

Do not confuse **tortuous** with **torturous**, which see.

Related words: **tortuosity** (TOR-choo-OS-i-tee) and **tortuousness** (TOR-choo-əs-nis) *both nouns,* **tortuously** *adverb.*

torturous (TOR-chər-əs) *adjective*
involving or causing torture or suffering; excruciating.

It is doubtful whether **tortuous** will ever recover from the ever-growing misuse of **torturous**, meaning *excruciating,* when a context calls for **tortuous**, meaning *full of twists and turns.* So painful is this misuse to anyone who values clear expression that not even permissive lexicographers are willing to bless this corruption. The message is clear: Be good to your editor and hold fast on the distinction between **tortuous** and **torturous**. No matter how **tortuous** your path through life, remember that *twists and turns* cannot break your bones, but **torturous** treatment by an alert and sadistic editor can be *excruciating.*

Related word: **torturously** *adverb.*

tractable (TRAK-tə-bəl) *adjective*
easy to manage or deal with; docile; manageable.

Related words: **tractability** (TRAK-tə-BIL-i-tee) and **tractableness** (TRAK-tə-bəl-nis) *both nouns,* **tractably** *adverb.*

traduce (trə-DOOS) *verb*
1. misrepresent.
2. slander; vilify.

Related words: **traducement** and **traducer** *both nouns,* **traducingly** *adverb.*

transcend (tran-SEND) *verb*
1. exceed in extent, degree, etc.; surpass.
2. excel.

3. go or be beyond the range of (human experience or belief or powers of description etc.).

Related words: **transcendence** (tran-SEN-dəns) and **transcendency** *both nouns,* **transcendingly** *adverb.*

translucent (trans-LOO-sənt) *adjective*
allowing light to pass through but not transparent.

Related words: **translucence** and **translucency** *both nouns,* **translucently** *adverb.*

transmute (trans-MYOOT) *verb*
cause to change in form or nature or substance; transform.

Related words: **transmutable** *adjective;* **transmutability** (trans-MYOOT-ə-BIL-i-tee), **transmutableness** (trans-MYOOT-ə-bəl-nis), and **transmuter** *all nouns;* **transmutably** *adverb.*

transpire (tran-SPĪR) *verb*
1. of information etc., be revealed, leak out, become known.
2. occur, take place, happen.
3. of plants, give off watery vapor from the surface of leaves etc.

Some writers do not use **transpire** in sense 2, *occur, happen,* given above. For example, they prefer to write "Something awful was about to happen" rather than "Something awful was about to transpire." Surely there is something to be said in favor of using the simpler word *happen* in such sentences, but there is nothing wrong with using **transpire** in this sense, as it has been for at least two centuries. And your readers will readily understand **transpire** used this way. So this is a case of you pays your money and you takes your choice.

Related words: **transpirable** (tran-SPĪR-ə-bəl) and **transpiratory** (tran-SPĪR-ə-TOR-ee) *both adjectives.*

trencherman (TREN-chər-mən) *noun, plural* **trenchermen**
1. a person who eats heartily.
2. a heavy eater.

triage (tree-AHZH) *noun*
1. the assignment of degrees of urgency to decide the order of treatment of people injured in a battle or disaster etc.
2. a selection system.

Related word: **triage** *adjective*, meaning *performing triage*.

troglodyte (TROG-lə-DĪT) *noun*
1. a cave dweller in prehistoric times; a caveman.
2. a person living in seclusion.
3. a hermit.

Related words: **troglodytic** (TROG-lə-DIT-ik) and **troglodytical** *both adjectives*, **troglodytism** (TROG-lə-dī-TIZ-əm) *noun*.

trollop (TROL-əp) *noun*
1. a promiscuous woman.
2. a prostitute; a slut.

Related word: **trollopy** *adjective*.

trope (trohp) *noun*
the use of a word in other than its literal sense; a figure of speech.

truculent (TRUK-yə-lənt) *adjective*
1. defiant and aggressive.
2. fierce, cruel.
3. pugnacious.

Related words: **truculence** and **truculency** *both nouns*, **truculently** *adverb*.

truism (TROO-iz-əm) *noun*
a self-evident, obvious truth; platitude.

Uninformed speakers and writers mistakenly use **truism** as a synonym for **truth**. As the definition above indicates, a **truism**, unlike **truth**, is seen as *self-evident, obvious*. Thus, **truism** is uncomplimentary, while **truth** surely is complimentary. So take care in keeping the two nouns distinct.

Related words: **truistic** (troo-IS-tik) and **truistical** *both adjectives*.

tsunami (tsuu-NAH-mee) *noun*
1. a series of huge sea waves caused by disturbance of the ocean floor or by seismic movement.
2. any comparably devastating force.

Related word: **tsunamic** (tsuu-NAH-mik) *adjective*.

turbid (TUR-bid) *adjective*
1. of liquids, muddy; thick; not clear.

2. unclear, obscure; confused; disordered.

Do not confuse **turbid** with **turgid**, which see.

Related words: **turbidity** (tur-BID-i-tee) and **turbidness** (TUR-bid-nis) *both nouns*, **turbidly** *adverb*.

turgid (TUR-jid) *adjective*

1. of language or style, pompous; overblown, grandiloquent; not flowing easily.
2. enlarged; swollen and not flexible.

In characterizing someone's literary style, do not confuse **turgid** in sense 1, *overblown, grandiloquent*, with **turbid** in sense 2, *unclear, obscure*. The spellings of these two adjectives invite confusion, and even knowledgable writers and editors fall into error. Again, **turgid** is somewhat more common than **turbid** and thus is likely to be used mistakenly when the sense of *unclear, obscure* is intended. To review the bidding: Remember that while **turgid** writing is properly thought of as *overblown* or *grandiloquent*, such writing may at the same time also be considered **turbid**, *unclear* or *obscure*. Yet, these two adjectives are clearly distinguishable from one another, and in your writing you must take care in using them, showing readers by your context which of the two derogatory meanings you intend. In fact, **turgid** writing is so often **turbid** that your task is not simple. Good luck.

Related words: **turgidity** (tur-JID-i-tee) and **turgidness** (TUR-jid-nis) *both nouns*, **turgidly** (TUR-jid-lee) *adverb*.

turpitude (TUR-pi-TOOD) *noun*

1. wickedness.
2. vileness; depravity.

tyrannicide (ti-RAN-ə-SĪD) *noun*

1. the act of killing a tyrant.
2. a person who commits tyrannicide.

Related word: **tyrannicidal** (ti-RAN-ə-SĪD-əl) *adjective*.

U

ubiquitous (yoo-BIK-wi-təs) *adjective*
being everywhere at the same time.
> Related words: **ubiquity** (yoo-BIK-wi-tee) and **ubiquitousness** *both nouns*, **ubiquitously** *adverb*.

ukase (yoo-KAYS) *noun*
1. an edict of the czarist Russian government.
2. an arbitrary order.

ultra vires (UL-trə VĪ-reez)
of a court or public official, beyond one's legal power or authority.

ululate (YOOL-yə-LAYT) *verb*
1. lament loudly and shrilly; wail.
2. howl; hoot.
> Related words: **ululant** (YOOL-yə-lənt) *adjective*, **ululation** (YOOL-yə-LAY-shən) *noun*.

umbrage (UM-brij) *noun*
a feeling of being offended.
> Related words: **umbrageous** (um-BRAY-jəs) *adjective*, **umbrageously** (um-BRAY-jəs-lee) *adverb*.

unbosom (un-BUUZ-əm) *verb*
disclose (a secret, a feeling, etc.), especially disclose one's opinions or thoughts in confidence.
> Related word: **unbosomer** (un-BUUZ-ə-mər) *noun*.

unconscionable (un-KON-shə-nə-bəl) *adjective*
1. unscrupulous.
2. contrary to what one's conscience feels is right.
3. outrageous.

Related words: **unconscionableness** *noun*, **unconscionably** *adverb*.

unction (UNGK-shən) *noun*
1. anointing with oil, especially as a religious rite.
2. pretended earnestness.
3. excessive politeness, especially in speaking.

unctuous (UNGK-choo-əs) *adjective*
1. having an oily manner.
2. smugly earnest or virtuous.

Related words: **unctuously** *adverb*, **unctuosity** (UNGK-choo-OS-i-tee) and **unctuousness** *both nouns*.

unequivocal (UN-i-KWIV-ə-kəl) *adjective*
clear and unmistakable; plain; unambiguous.

Related words: **unequivocally** *adverb*, **unequivocalness** *noun*.

unfledged (un-FLEJD) *adjective*
1. of a young bird, not yet able to fly; not fledged.
2. of a person, inexperienced.

uninterested (un-IN-tər-ə-stid) *adjective*
1. not interested.
2. showing or feeling no concern; indifferent.

See **disinterested** for guidance in the uses of **uninterested** and **disinterested**.

Related words: **uninterestedly** *adverb*, **uninterestedness** *noun*.

unjaundiced (un-JAWN-dist) *adjective*
free of distorted or prejudiced views.

unmitigated (un-MIT-i-GAY-tid) *adjective*
1. not modified.
2. unqualified; absolute.

Related word: **unmitigatedly** *adverb*.

unstudied (un-STUD-eed) *adjective*
1. natural in manner.
2. not affected; spontaneous.

untoward (un-TORD) *adjective*
1. inconvenient.
2. awkward.
3. refractory.
4. improper.
Related word: **untowardness** *noun*.

unwitting (un-WIT-ing) *adjective*
1. unaware.
2. unintentional.
Related words: **unwittingly** *adverb*, **unwittingness** *noun*.

urbane (ur-BAYN) *adjective*
having manners that are smooth and polite.
Related words: **urbanity** (ur-BAN-i-tee) and **urbaneness** (ur-BAYN-nis) *both nouns*, **urbanely** *adverb*.

ursine (UR-sīn) *adjective*
1. of or like a bear.
2. bearlike.

uxoricide (uk-SOR-ə-sīD) *noun*
1. the act of killing one's wife.
2. a person who commits uxoricide.
Related word: **uxoricidal** (uk-SOR-ə-SĪD-əl) *adjective*.

uxorious (uk-SOR-ee-əs) *adjective*
1. foolishly fond of one's wife.
2. of an action, showing such fondness.
Related words: **uxoriously** *adverb*, **uxoriousness** *noun*.

V

vacuous (VAK-yoo-əs) *adjective*
1. empty-headed; inane.
2. expressionless.

    Related words: **vacuity** (va-KYOO-i-tee) and **vacuousness** (VAK-yoo-əs-nis) *both nouns*, **vacuously** *adverb*.

vade mecum (VAY-dee MEE-kəm), *plural* **vade mecums**
1. a handbook or other small useful reference work a person carries with him.
2. a manual.

vagary (və-GAIR-ee *or* VAY-gə-ree) *noun, plural* **vagaries**
    a capricious act, idea, or fluctuation.

vainglory (VAYN-GLOR-ee) *noun*
1. boastfulness.
2. extreme vanity.

    Related words: **vainglorious** (vayn-GLOR-ee-əs) *adjective*, **vaingloriously** *adverb*, **vaingloriousness** *noun*.

valetudinarian (VAL-i-TOO-də-NAIR-ee-ən) *noun*, also given as **valetudinary** (VAL-i-TOO-də-NER-ee)
    a person who pays excessive attention to preserving his health.

    Related words: **valetudinary** *adjective*, **valetudinarianism** (VAL-i-TOO-də-NAIR-ee-ə-NIZ-əm) *noun*.

vapid (VAP-id) *adjective*
1. insipid; dull, uninteresting.

2. tedious.

Related words: **vapidity** (va-PID-i-tee) and **vapidness** (VAP-id-nis) *both nouns*, **vapidly** *adverb*.

variorum (VAIR-ee-OR-əm) *adjective*

with notes of various editors or commentators or with various versions of a text.

Related word: **variorum** *noun*, meaning *a variorum edition*.

venal (VEEN-əl) *adjective*

1. able to be bribed.
2. corruptible.
3. of conduct, influenced by bribery.

Do not confuse **venal** with **venial**, which see.

Related words: **venality** (vee-NAL-i-tee) *noun*, **venally** (VEEN-ə-lee) *adverb*.

venial (VEE-nee-əl) *adjective*

1. of a fault or sin, pardonable.
2. of misconduct, trifling, not serious.

Some writers and speakers confuse **venial**, meaning *trifling* or *pardonable*, with **venal**, meaning *corruptible*. Since these words are so far apart in meaning, this confusion seems to be caused solely by the closeness in spelling of the two words. Although this sin of confusion by writers and readers may be **venial**, or *pardonable*, most of us believe **venality**, or *corruptibility*, is never pardonable. Let us resolve, therefore, to do our best (1) to overcome even *trivial*, or **venial**, personal faults and (2) to avoid **venality**, or *corruptibility*, completely by eschewing any behavior that may be characterized as **venal**.

Related words: **veniality** (VEE-nee-AL-i-tee) and **venialness** (VEE-nee-əl-nis) *both nouns*, **venially** *adverb*.

veracious (və-RAY-shəs) *adjective*

1. truthful, honest.
2. true.

Related words: **veraciousness** and **veracity** (və-RAS-i-tee) *both nouns*, **veraciously** *adverb*.

verbiage (VUR-bee-ij) *noun*

an excessive number of words used to express an idea; verbosity.

verbicide (VUR-bə-SĪD) *noun*
1. the destruction of the sense or value of a word.
2. one who willfully commits verbicide.

verbose (vər-BOHS) *adjective*
using more words than are needed; prolix; long-winded.
Related words: **verboseness** and **verbosity** (vər-BOS-i-tee) *both nouns*, **verbosely** *adverb*.

veridical (və-RID-i-kəl) *adjective*, also given as **veridic** (və-RID-ik)
1. truthful, veracious.
2. genuine.
Related words: **veridicality** (və-RID-i-KAL-i-tee) *noun*, **veridically** (və-RID-i-kə-lee) *adverb*.

verisimilitude (VER-ə-si-MIL-i-TOOD) *noun*
1. an appearance of being true.
2. likelihood, probability.

veritable (VER-i-tə-bəl) *adjective*
1. real.
2. rightly named.
Related words: **veritableness** *noun*, **veritably** *adverb*.

vernacular (vər-NAK-yə-lər) *noun*
1. the language or dialect of a country.
2. the everyday speech of ordinary people.
Related words: **vernacular** *adjective*, **vernacularly** *adverb*.

viable (VĪ-ə-bəl) *adjective*
1. practicable.
2. able to exist successfully.
3. of a fetus, sufficiently developed to be able to survive after birth.
4. of plants, able to live or grow.
Related words: **viability** (VĪ-ə-BIL-i-tee) *noun*, **viably** (VĪ-ə-blee) *adverb*.

vicarious (vī-KAR-ee-əs) *adjective*
of feelings or emotions, felt through sharing imaginatively in the feelings or emotions of another person.
Related words: **vicariously** *adverb*, **vicariousness** *noun*.

vicissitude (vi-SIS-i-TOOD) *noun*
a change of circumstances affecting one's life.

Related words: **vicissitudinary** (vi-SIS-i-TOO-də-NER-ee) and **vicissitudinous** (vi-SIS-i-TOO-də-nəs) *both adjectives.*

vincible (VIN-sə-bəl) *adjective*
that can be overcome or conquered.

Related words: **vincibility** (VIN-si-BIL-i-tee) and **vincibleness** (VIN-sə-bəl-nis) *both nouns.*

virago (vi-RAH-goh) *noun, plural* **viragoes** and **viragos**
a shrewish bullying woman; a scold; a termagant.

Related words: **viraginian** (VIR-ə-JIN-ee-ən) and **viraginous** (vi-RAJ-ə-nəs) *both adjectives,* **viraginity** (VIR-ə-JIN-i-tee) *noun.*

viscid (VIS-id) *adjective*
of liquid, thick and sticky; viscous.

Related words: **viscidity** (vi-SID-i-tee) and **viscidness** (VIS-id-nis) *both nouns,* **viscidly** *adverb.*

viscous (VIS-kəs) *adjective*
of liquid, not pouring easily; thick and sticky.

Related words: **viscosity** (vi-SKOS-i-tee) and **viscousness** *both nouns,* **viscously** *adverb.*

vitiate (VISH-ee-AYT) *verb*
1. impair the quality of; debase.
2. make ineffectual; weaken; invalidate.

Related words: **vitiable** (VISH-ee-ə-bəl) *adjective,* **vitiation** (VISH-ee-AY-shən) and **vitiator** (VISH-ee-AY-tər) *both nouns.*

vituperate (vī-TOO-pə-RAYT) *verb*
use abusive language; abuse; objurgate, revile.

Related words: **vituperation** (vī-TOO-pə-RAY-shən) and **vituperator** (vī-TOO-pər-AY-tər) *both nouns,* **vituperative** (vī-TOO-pər-ə-tiv) *adjective,* **vituperatively** *adverb.*

viva voce (VĪ-və VOH-see)
1. a university examination conducted orally.
2. the oral part of a university examination.

3. **viva-voce** (VĪ-və-VOH-see) *adjective*, of such an examination, conducted orally; spoken not written.

viviparous (vi-VIP-ər-əs) *adjective*
1. bringing forth young alive, not hatching by means of an egg.
2. producing bulbs or seeds that germinate while still attached to the parent plant.

Related words: **viviparism** (vi-VIP-ə-riz-əm), **viviparity** (VIV-ə-PAR-i-tee), **viviparousness** (vi-VIP-ər-əs-nis) *all nouns*; **viviparously** *adverb*.

vociferate (voh-SIF-ə-RAYT) *verb*
1. speak or say loudly or noisily.
2. shout.

Related words: **vociferant** (voh-SIF-ə-rənt) *adjective* and *noun*, **vociferation** (voh-SIF-ə-RAY-shən) *noun*, **vociferous** (voh-SIF-ə-rəs) *adjective*, **vociferousness** *noun*.

volatile (VOL-ə-til) *adjective*
1. of a person, lively.
2. of a person, changing quickly or easily from one mood or interest to another.
3. of a liquid, evaporating quickly.

Related words: **volatility** (VOL-ə-TIL-i-tee) and **volatileness** *both nouns*.

volition (voh-LISH-ən) *noun*
use of one's own will in choosing or making a decision etc.

Related words: **volitional** and **volitionary** (voh-LISH-ə-NER-ee) *both adjectives*, **volitionally** *adverb*.

volte-face (volt-FAHS) *noun, plural* **volte-face**
1. a complete change of one's attitude toward something.
2. a reversal of opinion; a turnabout.

voluble (VOL-yə-bəl) *adjective*
1. talking very much.
2. speaking or spoken with great fluency.

Related words: **volubility** (VOL-yə-BIL-i-tee) and **volubleness** (VOL-yə-bəl-nis) *both nouns*, **volubly** *adverb*.

voluptuary (və-LUP-choo-ER-ee) *noun, plural* **voluptuaries**
a person whose life is devoted to indulgence in luxury and sensual pleasure; a sybarite.

voracious (vaw-RAY-shəs) *adjective*
1. greedy in eating; gluttonous.
2. ravenous.
3. insatiable.

Related words: **voracity** (vaw-RAS-i-tee) and **voraciousness** (vaw-RAY-shəs-nis) *both nouns,* **voraciously** *adverb.*

vouchsafe (vowch-SAYF) *verb*
give or grant in a gracious or condescending manner.

Related word: **vouchsafement** (vowch-SAYF-mənt) *noun.*

voyeur (vwah-YUR) *noun*
a person who obtains sexual gratification from observing the sexual actions or organs of others, especially secretively.

Related words: **voyeurism** (vwah-YUR-iz-əm) *noun,* **voyeuristic** (VWAH-yə-RIS-tik) *adjective,* **voyeuristically** *adverb.*

vulpine (VUL-pīn) *adjective*
1. of or like a fox.
2. crafty, cunning.

W

wanton (WON-tən) *adjective*
1. lacking proper restraint or motives.
2. irresponsible.
   Related words: **wantonly** *adverb*, **wantonness** *noun*.

waspish (WOS-pish) *adjective*
1. sharp in retort.
2. ill-tempered, irascible.
   Related words: **waspishly** *adverb*, **waspishness** *noun*.

wastrel (WAY-strəl) *noun*
a wasteful person, especially one who wastes money; a spendthrift.

watershed (WAW-tər-SHED) *noun*
1. a turning point in the course of events.
2. a region drained by a river or river system.

weir (weer) *noun*
1. a small dam built across a river or stream so that water flows over it, serving to regulate the flow or to raise the level of water upstream.
2. a fence, as of brushwood or stakes with nets, built in a stream or channel to catch fish.

wheedle (HWEE-dəl) *verb*
1. coax.
2. persuade or obtain by coaxing.
   Related words: **wheedler** *noun*, **wheedlingly** *adverb*.

whet (hwet) *verb*
1. sharpen (a tool etc.) by rubbing against an abrasive stone etc.
2. stimulate; make keen or eager.

Related word: **whetter** *noun*.

willful (WIL-fəl) *adjective*
1. done with deliberate intention and not by accident.
2. self-willed; obstinate; headstrong.

Related words: **willfully** *adverb*, **willfulness** (WIL-fəl-nis) *noun*.

winnow (WIN-oh) *verb*
1. expose (grain) to a current of air by tossing or fanning (the grain) so that the loose dry outer part is blown away.
2. separate (chaff) in this way.
3. sift or separate (worthwhile material) from worthless or inferior material.

Related word: **winnower** *noun*.

wont (wawnt *or* wohnt) *noun*
1. a habit, practice, or custom.
2. (*adjective*) accustomed.

Related word: **wontless** *adjective*.

wreak (reek) *verb*
1. inflict.
2. cause.

Related word: **wreaker** *noun*.

wunderkind (VUUN-dər-KIND) *noun, plural* **wunderkinds**, *German plural* **Wunderkinder** (VUUN-dər-KIND-ər)
1. a child prodigy.
2. a person who achieves great success, especially in business, while relatively young.

XYZ

Xanthippe (zan-TIP-ee) *noun,* also given as **Xantippe**
a shrew, especially a shrewish wife; a scold.

yahoo (YAH-hoo) *noun, plural* **yahoos**
1. a coarse or brutish person; a lout.
2. a philistine; a yokel.
    Related word: **yahooism** (YAH-hoo-iz-əm) *noun.*

yarmulke (YAHR-məl-kə) *noun,* also given as **yarmelke** and **yarmulka,**
with the same pronunciation
a skullcap worn by male Orthodox and Conservative Jews, especially in a synagogue and during prayers.

yclept (ee-KLEPT) *adjective*
called (by the name of).

yeasty (YEE-stee) *adjective*
1. tasting of yeast.
2. frothy, foamy.
3. light and superficial; frivolous.
4. very enthusiastic or joyful.
    Related words: **yeastily** (YEE-sti-lee) *adverb,* **yeastiness** *noun.*

zealot (ZEL-ət) *noun*
1. a zealous person.
2. a fanatic.
    Related word: **zealotry** (ZEL-ə-tree) *noun.*

zealous (ZEL-əs) *adjective*
> 1. full of fervor for a person, a cause, or an object.
> 2. devoted, diligent.
>
> Related words: **zealously** *adverb*, **zealousness** *noun*.

Zeitgeist (TSĪT-GĪST) *noun*, German
> the trend of thought and feeling in a period of time.

zucchetto (zoo-KET-oh) *noun, plural* **zucchettos** or **zucchetti** (zoo-KET-ee)
> in the Roman Catholic Church, an ecclesiastical skullcap, black for a priest, violet for a bishop, red for a cardinal, and white for the pope.